Strategic Affiliate Marketing

Strategic Affiliate Marketing

Simon Goldschmidt
TradeDoubler, Copenhagen, Denmark

Sven Junghagen
Department of Management, Politics and Philosophy,
Copenhagen Business School, Denmark

Uri Harris
McKinsey & Co., Copenhagen, Denmark

Edward Elgar
Cheltenham, UK • Northampton, MA, USA

Published by
Edward Elgar Publishing Limited
Glensanda House
Montpellier Parade
Cheltenham
Glos GL50 1UA
UK

Edward Elgar Publishing, Inc.
136 West Street
Suite 202
Northampton
Massachusetts 01060
USA

A catalogue record for this book
is available from the British Library

Library of Congress Cataloguing in Publication Data

Goldschmidt, Simon, 1974-
    Strategic affiliate marketing / Simon Goldschmidt, Sven Junghagen, Uri Harris
    p. cm.
    Includes bibliographical references.
    1. Multilevel marketing. 2. Business Networks. 3. Internet Marketing. I.
Junghagen, Sven, 1964- II. Harris, Uri, 1976- III. Title.

HF5415. 126.G65 2003
658.8'4—dc21

2003046378

ISBN 1 84376 390 7

Printed and bound in Great Britain by MPG Books Ltd, Bodmin, Cornwall

Contents

v

Preface

Even though it can be argued that affiliate marketing is an old phenomenon in a rapidly changing online business environment, it is still a new and developing business area in the sense that marketers, media, e-consultants, media agencies and other players in affiliate marketing are only in the process of establishing a sustainable level of activities in this specific business area. In addition, due to natural variations in online objectives, profit margins, functionalities, foci, target groups, and needs of communication, each industry is adopting affiliate marketing in a separate and unique conduct.

The contribution of this book is a theoretical approach of how to act in an affiliate network taking into account the characteristics of the Internet and interactions among participants. Various set-ups of a new and focused marketing phenomenon are weighed against both established and new marketing and strategy theories. Without arguing for any absolute answers as to what is right and wrong, this book aims at analysing how a participant can engage in affiliate marketing, and what should be considered before becoming active and once active, how to optimise resources.

TradeDoubler is delivering tracking technology and solutions to various online business activities. However, with the focus of this book, we have purely used TradeDoubler as a case study for the purpose of explaining and researching the value creation and strategic considerations in affiliate marketing. Thus, we would like to thank TradeDoubler for providing us with useful insights, which have allowed us to compose an in-depth analysis balancing practical and theoretical discussions.

This book provides constructive information and perspectives for affiliates and marketers who are active in affiliate marketing, as well as those who are considering becoming involved in it. Moreover, because of the balance between theoretical and practical analysis the book is suitable for individuals with an academic and intellectual interest in the area of online marketing.

About the authors

Simon Goldschmidt, MSc in International Marketing Management, Country Manager, TradeDoubler, has been working with the sales, consulting, and administration of affiliate marketing on a European level since 2000. He is also co-chairman of the Danish e-business Associations Marketing Department. Simon is an active speaker in the area of online marketing and online return on investment. His work is primarily motivated by a profound interest in how various businesses and industries can exploit and optimise their commercial interests on the Internet.

Sven Junghagen, PhD, Associate Professor in Strategic Management at the Department of Management, Politics and Philosophy, Copenhagen Business School, has been studying the relation between strategic management and information technologies since the mid 1990s. He has been functioning as an expert for the Swedish Business Development Agency and for the European Commission, DG Information Society. He is a board member of firms and organisations such as the World Internet Institute. He is affiliated to the Scandinavian Academy of Management Studies where he is the director of the research programme MICT – Management of Information and Communication Technologies – and responsible for the project E-learning Øresund. Being a Swede living in Sweden and working in Denmark, he sees himself as a living example of the trend of transnational regionalisation.

Uri Harris, MSc, Associate at McKinsey & Company's Copenhagen office, has worked with a number of Scandinavian clients on strategic management issues, both in his current position and previously at Danish strategy consulting firm Lund-Andersen. He is co-founder of a 'New Economy' consulting firm, having experienced the ups and downs involved in such a venture through a rapidly shifting economic environment. Currently working mainly with clients outside the IT industry, Uri's focus is not on information technology per se, but rather on studying how companies can achieve strong performance through a variety of strategic and operational tools, of which information technology is one. In his spare time, convinced that he has personally realised only a fraction of the potential information technology has to offer, Uri is working hard on making the transition to a fully-fledged member of the Internet Age.

PART I

The Basics of Internet Marketing

The Basics of Internet Marketing

The aim of this first part is to set the scene for this book on strategic affiliate marketing. We have all, in some way, been confronted with arguments claiming that the new economy, the information society and electronic commerce will have a huge impact on our lives as consumers. Because of the technological possibilities, it is possible for marketers to address an extensive array of customers and to create new business in an evolving market space. The first attempts to shape the logics of advertising on the Internet extrapolated the revenue models from advertising in the 'physical world'. These advertising efforts tended though to be inefficient and so performance-based revenue models evolved as a consequence.

Affiliate marketing is a principle based on these new revenue models and these principles will be introduced in this first part. Even though the problem with inefficient communication channels is solved, there is still one fundamental issue to be considered in order to be successful in Internet Marketing – an understanding of Internet customers. These issues are dealt with in Chapter 2, which is a discussion of the behaviour of both consumers and business customers.

1. Internet – A New Marketing Arena

The aim of this introductory chapter is to give a brief picture of Internet marketing, as it emerged during the second half of the 1990s. Even though a discussion on the new economy and Internet marketing is much broader than the concept of affiliate marketing, we start here to understand the context wherein affiliate marketing takes place. There is a difference in business logic between affiliate marketing and traditional advertising even on the Internet. These basic principles will be accounted for to provide the reader with a foundation for the remaining chapters.

1.1 THE NEW ECONOMY: MYTH OR FACT?

The notion of the new economy has become a widespread and widely used concept, even though we may not know what it actually is. An ongoing discourse during the last decade has announced an 'IT-revolution', the transition from the industrial to the information society where the main goods will be information rather than physically manufactured goods. The question of whether this conception is true or not will be left unanswered here but we will settle for an account of the discourse on the new economy. A complete discussion on this topic would in fact take up a book on its own.

One commonly used milestone in the narrative of the emergent 'IT-revolution' was when the prime minister of Sweden, Carl Bildt sent his first e-mail to President Bill Clinton in 4 February 1994. Here is an excerpt from that e-mail (The Knowledge Foundation, 2001):

> Dear Bill, Apart from testing this connection on the global Internet system... Sweden is – as you know – one of the leading countries in the world in the field of telecommunications, and it is only appropriate that we should be among the first to use the Internet also for political contacts and communications around the globe. Yours, Carl

In this new millennium we take this kind of communication for granted but back in 1994 it was not that obvious that two heads of state should use e-mail for their correspondence. This is just one anecdotal example and there are lots more of them. Each and every one might not be important but they all contributed to a discourse strengthening the mythological notion of the new economy.

The emergence of e-commerce and e-business during the second half of
the 1990s is another tendency often used as an indicator of a new economy.
The fact is that these phenomena as such are not especially new, since firms
have been using information and communication technologies for a long time
in order to deal with business transactions. An example of this is EDI
(Electronic Data Interchange) systems that have been used in business-to-
business markets. The main development of e-commerce and e-business by
means of the Internet is the possibility of addressing a larger number of
single customers with a higher level of communication quality than before.
According to Evans and Wurster (1997), the elimination of trade-off between
richness and reach might be the most important issue in the information
economy. In 'traditional' mass communication media this trade-off means
that you cannot have a rich communication and at the same time reach a high
number of parties.

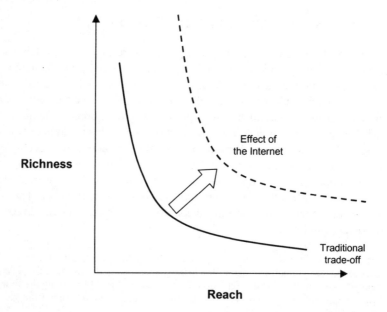

Source: Evans and Wurster, 1997

Figure 1.1   The blow-up of the richness/reach trade-off

As illustrated in Figure 1.1, any given choice between richness and reach is
limited to the curve showing the traditional correlation between richness and
reach. The effect of the Internet is that a communicative effort is no longer

limited to the curve since increased connectivity and the development of common communication standards has meant that the curve can be moved.

The question is then, whether or not we are experiencing a new economy today. Well, it all depends on how we define the 'new' in the new economy. Even though we might have access to new technologies, enabling communication patterns that were not dreamt of a decade ago, the basic premises for business are still the same. As Shapiro and Varian (1999) put it: 'Technology changes. Economic laws do not'.

There are a number of issues raised by Shapiro and Varian, to prove that you do not need new economics to understand the new economy. Without going into all these, we would like to point out the most important reason for believing that traditional strategy and marketing virtues are still valid. At the end of the day, the most fundamental reason-to-be for firms is that they are able to provide a value for someone outside the firm and that this someone is willing to pay for this value at a profitable price for the firm. During the years 2000 and 2001, many so-called dot.coms have experienced extreme difficulties and have eventually failed. There have been many different arguments why these firms could not survive; one commonly used argument has been that consumers were not ready to adopt the technological possibilities. Another argument has been the lack of sophistication and consistency in interfaces. These arguments all take their point of departure in a technological imperative, meaning that if technology enables you to confront many customers you should also be able to sell a lot. The basic problem is, however, that you have to be able to provide something that is perceived as valuable in order to survive on a long-term basis.

There are, however, some basics of strategy and marketing that are affected by the emergence of electronic business on the Internet. In spite of this fact we can still find texts discussing the marketing mix on the Internet, as it was proposed by McCarthy (1960). The 4Ps model of Product, Place, Promotion and Price has been dominant in marketing since it was introduced in the early 1960s. A dominant part of the literature on Internet marketing still takes as its point of departure this generic conception of the marketing mix. As a short reflection based on the aforementioned possibilities of changing communicative patterns we can see some immediate effects of the Internet on the marketing mix concept.

The elements of the marketing mix should all contribute to the fulfilment of marketing strategies. The elements are quite separable and can be planned more or less independently of each other. The effect of the Internet is that the boundaries between these elements are blurred to some extent. An Internet website can function as the place, the product and the promotion at the same time. The main question for future marketing should therefore not be what product in what place for what price, but rather what kind of value do we produce for someone who is willing to pay for it?

Even though we cannot state whether we truly experience a new economy, and we do not have the ambition to attempt to give an answer, we do experience some basic changes in the way we can approach customers with a value proposition.

1.2   A NEW BUSINESS LOGIC?

Even though one might agree with Shapiro and Varian that technology changes but economic laws do not, there are some new tendencies that can be observed.

The Internet as a Platform

Many businesses have been working in a digital environment for quite some time already. There have been some problems though in terms of possibilities to create new business on these technological platforms. In the age of EDI all applications were quite platform dependent and information systems were tailored to the specific firms involved in the network. Most often these information systems functioned as a lock-in of subcontractors to a larger firm. The systems were closed so the potential to attract new customers was not present. Furthermore, there was a need for development of standards in order to open up the systems to new entrants (Junghagen, 1995).

The emergence of commercial use of the Internet seemed to have the potential to overcome these issues, mainly because the Internet possesses the following characteristics (Bennett, 2001). It is:

- Interactive (so that products can be offered and orders transacted in the same environment)
- Switched (so different business transactions can be conducted with different customers simultaneously)
- Broadband (so that those offers can be communicated in an engaging and attractive mode)
- Networked (so that product offers, orders, shipping, inventory, and accounting can be integrated)
- Standards-based (It is platform-independent, so that everyone can get to it).

These characteristics have created possibilities to organise business models that were impossible in the 'pre-Internet era'. The fundamental business logic is still there, the one about providing value to someone outside the firm who is willing to pay for it, but some roles and activities in an economic system can be changed. In the following we will account for the obsolescence of the marketing mix, changes in marketing communication systems and the dissolving value chains.

The Obsolescence of the Marketing Mix

In a traditional marketing mix perspective it is possible to define boundaries between the elements. There is also a clear conception of a means–ends hierarchy where corporate and business strategies are broken down into functional strategies and marketing operations. The reason for dividing the activities into elements of a mix is basically the fact that in traditional marketing the product is one entity, distribution of this product another, and communications with the market a third. The marketing mix concept has been the subject of criticism since its introduction. The main reason for this is that it does not take all relevant factors into account and the consequence has been that more Ps have been added or that alternative perspectives have evolved. It is not our intention to go deep into this discussion but rather illuminate our view of how the Internet affects the marketing mix perspective.

First of all we can see a blurring of boundaries between the elements since a site on the Internet can function as a communications medium, as a platform for transaction, as the distribution system and even as the product itself, and all of this at the same time. This means that the planning of the marketing mix might no longer be a series of decisions, made in isolation even though they are interrelated, but rather a complex decision situation where one decision might affect most elements of the traditional marketing mix.

Second, another effect is that 'operational' marketing has to be entered into the strategic agenda even more than before. A traditionally operational decision will have even more strategic consequences, if the operation is carried out on the Internet, because of the transparency and the immediate effect on the firm's environment.

Another important effect is that we have to reassess what factors and variables to measure and analyse when stating communication objectives. When using traditional communications media, objectives should be formulated in terms of communicative effects, level of desired change, in a specific target audience, during a specific time period (Colley, 1961). On the Internet, the objectives involved in using a certain communications medium can go beyond the actual communications effects since the medium can function as more than a vehicle for communication. This effect is basically the rationale of this book. Since it is possible to redefine the way to set communication objectives one can also redefine revenue models for marketing communication media. New revenue models and new business models will in turn affect the roles and activities in the relations between actors in marketing communication systems.

Marketing Communication Systems

As has been stated above the marketing mix and the inseparability between the elements in the mix might be obsolete on the Internet. This will affect the system of actors involved in marketing communications. Although it is fairly obvious that the communications medium should be regarded as the vehicle for communications it may at the same time be the appropriate sales channel as well. If we turn that around a sales channel could also be an appropriate communications medium.

From the customer's point of view it might be so that he or she would like to have the exchange with the medium since they have an established relationship. Even though this exchange just might not be real since the actual transaction is linked to the marketer it might make sense to the consumer. These effects on marketing communication systems will be further elaborated upon in Chapter 2.

What About the Value Chain?

The above discussions indicate that the conception of value chains (Porter, 1980) might also be obsolete to some extent since activities and roles in the value creation process seem to be changing. This possible development can be illuminated by the following example.

In a traditional setting a producer of a certain good sells this to the retailer through wholesalers. The retailers have products in stock and sell these to consumers. The core competence for the retailer is commerce, selling products to consumers. As was stated above, the communications media would then function as a supporting service in the value chain but not contribute directly to value creation. This traditional setting can be seen in Figure 1.2.

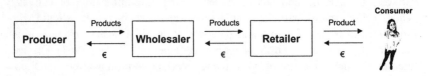

Figure 1.2   A traditional value chain in retailing

Now imagine a setting on the Internet. A consumer wants to buy a certain product from a retailer's website. The consumer finds the desired product and buys it on that site. However, this retailer does not hold stock and does not sell anything. Instead, the consumer has bought the product directly from the producer and the retailer gets a commission for handling the transaction. The core competences of the retailer are here to have an understanding of the needs in the market, put together an assortment, and to intermediate between the producer and the consumer. This imaginary system is illustrated in Figure 1.3.

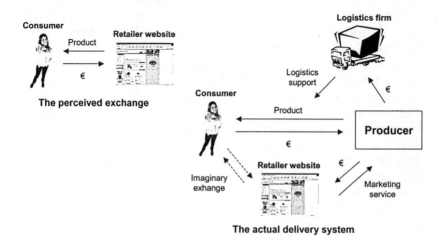

Figure 1.3   An imaginary delivery system

This is not a new phenomenon since commission-based sales have existed for a long time. It is though, much more convenient to handle these situations in a digital setting than in a physical setting. In a physical setting a retailer has to have products physically located in store in order to intermediate the sale, but in a digital setting the retailer is virtual and the consumer expects the product to be delivered by a third party anyway.

The implication is that we have to accept that the traditional value chain might change where we experience a blurring of boundaries between value activities and supporting activities. This merger between retailing and advertising media is the foundation for affiliate marketing on the Internet, which will be introduced in the coming sections.

1.3 ADVERTISING ON THE INTERNET – A RETROSPECTION

The development of the Internet as a potential arena for marketing has been intense from about 1995 onward. Even though the Internet is not an especially new phenomenon the potential for marketing did not really occur until the introduction of graphical interfaces by means of the World Wide Web. The Internet was shortly after heralded as the ultimate marketing tool. Its user base grew dramatically, and the idea was that any person could communicate with any other person instantly and at essentially no costs (Evans and Wurster, 1997). More and more companies put up websites and started sending out e-mails, and companies like Amazon.com were seen by many to set entirely new standards for customer marketing (Spector, 2000). Traditional companies and online businesses alike invested heavily in developing Internet tools for sales and marketing. This raised expectations for the new medium to astronomical levels. After some time, however, it became clear that for many companies the expectations were not being met. The proliferation of websites led users to experience even more information overload than before, and companies had to spend huge sums on online and offline advertising to overshadow other companies and get potential customers to their sites. Naturally, this led to very high acquisition costs for each customer (Lindstrom, 2001). At the same time, online advertising, which consisted almost entirely of banners, became less and less effective over time. Online users simply learned to ignore them, and their click-through rates fell on average to well below 1 per cent (IDC, 1999; Bruner et al., 2001).

The question then was how to utilise this new medium to sell and market products and services to customers. Few people question that the Internet offers advantages that no other medium can. In particular, it allows for two-way communication giving the possibility of interaction between company and customer. As a way to promote this type of interaction, online 'communities' have been focused on as a major step in that direction (Armstrong and Hagel, 1996; Hagel and Armstrong, 1997). Since it is so cheap and easy to publish information on the Internet it would seem that people would gather in small communities of interest within very narrow areas where firms can reach them with relevant marketing.

In many ways, however, the proliferation of small, niche websites made marketing and advertising more difficult. With literally millions of websites, marketers have difficulty comprehending the entire picture. Currently, there are more than nine million commercial websites registered (Bruner et al., 2001). This makes it difficult for marketers to get their message out to users. What has happened is that the vast majority of advertising revenue has gone to the very large websites, such as Yahoo and AOL. In 1999, 71 per cent of all advertising spending went to the fifteen largest websites (Jupiter Communications, 2000a). The important rationale for this imbalance was that advertisers at least knew that they were getting reach in terms of number of consumers exposed to the message. The problem with this imbalance is that online advertising became static and unfocused. Markets were not targeted properly, without any significant segmentation efforts from marketers. Rather than utilising the unique possibilities of the Internet, it actually became less effective than offline marketing.

At the same time, the smaller-sized websites that were not generating much advertising revenue opted to join advertising networks such as DoubleClick, which packaged smaller websites together, making it easier for marketers to reach a more targeted audience, while saving them searching costs. However, this did not solve the problem, as online advertising effectiveness continued to drop and advertising rates fell sharply (Bruner et al., 2001). Typically, even leading Internet advertising networks sell only 5–7.5 per cent of their inventory at premium prices, with the rest being disposed at an extremely low CPM (cost per thousand impressions) rate of down to $1 (Barsh et al., 2001). An estimated 70–80 per cent of websites' inventory of advertising space remains completely unused (Bruner et al., 2001). Thus, marketers were unhappy because their marketing money was ineffective, websites were unhappy because the advertising prices fell steeply, and consumers were unhappy because they were bombarded with irrelevant advertising. Perhaps a new method was required? Several new methods/tools for online marketing were developed quite early, and the most effective of them gained stature over time.

1.4 AN INTRODUCTION TO AFFILIATE MARKETING

Affiliate marketing originates from Amazon.com's introduction of partnership- and commission-based marketing in July 1996. Amazon discovered this new marketing approach when contacted by a woman who wanted commissions on the customers she was referring. This woman had a website with cookery recipes, and many of her visitors had asked her where they could find good cookbooks. She had been recommending that they go to Amazon to buy them, which many of them did. After a while, she contacted Amazon and asked for commission for leading potential customers to the firm via her website. This was the beginning of affiliate marketing for Amazon, who caught on to this idea and started to offer other websites an affiliation (partnership) with the firm and a commission on sales generated via their website (Helmstetter and Metivier, 2000; Kjærsdam, 2000).

Currently, Amazon has approximately 400,000 affiliated websites (Bruner et al., 2001).

Other online retailers followed Amazon's example, and there are now well over one thousand affiliate marketing programmes in existence (Silverstein, 2001). However, due to the amount of administration in terms of support, segmentation, and payments to many thousands of affiliates as well as the need for a continuous technological development, the foundation was created for a separate industry, where marketers outsource their affiliate marketing needs to specialized 'brokers' that handle programmes for many marketers (IDC, 1999). Nonetheless, the principles of the business models are somewhat similar. The user is exposed to a product or a service in the context of the environment he or she is in, when using the Internet, and the marketer pays the affiliate based on predefined performance criteria. In the USA, there are several brokers that run affiliate marketing programmes for marketers, and in Europe there are a few, of which one, TradeDoubler, is the largest. TradeDoubler's European affiliate marketing network consists of more than 400,000 participants, of which about 500 are marketers. The TradeDoubler Affiliate Marketing Programme will serve as a case throughout this book.

Given the growth and increased adoption of affiliate marketing over the past few years, it appears to be taking an important role in the future development of sales and marketing on the Internet, an area which itself has been attributed with high future expectations (Jupiter Communications, 2000a; Bruner et al., 2001). The discourse so far on affiliate marketing has mostly focused on the accountability of marketing expenditures in a performance-based payment structure (e.g. Silverstein, 2001; Jupiter Communications, 1998b; IDC, 1999). Marketers are able to control advertising expenditures and only pay for attention instead of exposure. This is undoubtedly attractive for online marketers and an important reason for the growth of affiliate marketing, but there is indication that affiliate marketing is much broader in scope. For example, a Forrester Research (1999) study found that click-through rates for affiliate marketing links were six times higher than click-through rates for ad banners. This is explained because of small niche affiliates' ability to provide users with more relevant marketing messages than larger websites that typically carry banner ads. This issue, and others, indicates that there is more to affiliate marketing than marketing accountability, although it is an important part of it.

Furthermore, while many online marketers have found affiliate marketing attractive, others have complained over its lack of effectiveness (Cotlier, 2001). This implies that at least for some marketers, it may not be a panacea for online marketing. Additionally, some websites (and their representative agencies) have expressed resentment over the performance-based payment structure, accusing it of being exploitative and 'killing off' websites (e.g. Neubert, 2000). The performance-based payment structure does represent a significant change in the revenue model for media firms, seen in relation to the previously widespread impression-based advertising model, and this may have significant strategic implications for these firms. Affiliate marketing is still a relatively new phenomenon, and some of the implications of using it may only now be emerging, as firms adopt it on a larger scale.

A basic assumption is that for something like this to work, there are certain requirements in the marketplace that need to be met. While hype and bandwagon effects can drive growth in the short term, in the longer term affiliate marketing must offer real value to its participants. As with most initiatives, the actual extent of this value depends on the situation of the specific firm in question, but there should at least be some potential benefits that firms can evaluate in relation to their own situation. Undoubtedly, affiliate marketing has strategic implications for its participants, which may go beyond the initial benefits. Hence, the strategic implications of participation are an important part of any evaluation.

In an affiliate network, there are a number of actors and relations. The most important one is the relationship between the marketer and the customer. Without this relation, everything else will fall apart. Dependent on the specific situation, the marketer might have one or more objectives with an online communication effort. It might be to expose an offer to customers, to get recognition for a brand or products, to shape or change attitudes or to stimulate an exchange of some kind. Instead of handling this communication by itself, the marketer involves the affiliate in the process, and the affiliate gets its revenues based on the performance. Roughly speaking, this performance is to create attention, interest, desire and/or action. A model is shown in Figure 1.4 showing combinations of objectives and performance and how these are measured.

Affiliate marketing does not always mean that an affiliate gets a commission on direct sales. The measure used for revenues is dependent on communication objectives for the marketer and expected performance of the affiliate. These dimensions are in turn affected by the communication problem at hand, defined by an understanding of customers, their preferences and their behaviour.

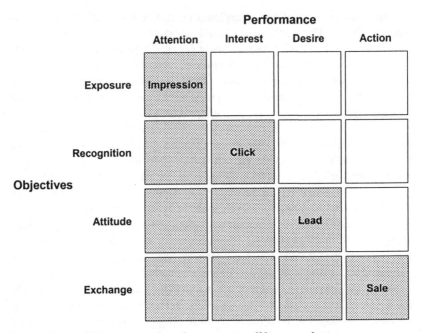

Figure 1.4   Objectives and performance in affiliate marketing

1.5   THE AIM OF THE BOOK

The aim of this book is to address the issue of changing roles in the e-commerce area. As has been stated, the basic effects of the Internet on economic activity have been the changing roles of actors, the blurring of boundaries in the marketing mix, and finally as a consequence, the changing business models from exposure-based to performance-based revenue models for marketing communications. The primary focus of the book is on performance-based revenue models – affiliate marketing. There are three main questions answered, and these questions can be structured so they are read as a sequential process, where the output of one serves as (partial) input for the next:

- What is affiliate marketing, and in which context does it occur?
- Why is affiliate marketing an attractive option for participants?
- Which considerations should firms go through in determining the potential use of affiliate marketing?

We build our discussion around answering each of these questions in turn, as they each provide an important piece of the puzzle. Below is an elaboration of how we interpret each question, and how we intend to address it.

What is Affiliate Marketing, and in Which Context Does it Occur?

We base our initial understanding of affiliate marketing on the basic principles presented in the previous section. However, the phenomenon cannot be separated from the context in which it occurs. In order to identify the value of affiliate marketing and determine strategic considerations for participants, it is necessary to first understand the structure and processes that underlie it. As mentioned earlier, affiliate marketing takes place in a network of firms. A more elaborate description of participants' roles and transaction processes in this network is necessary as a foundation for further research.

Why is Affiliate Marketing an Attractive Option for Participants?

In order for affiliate marketing to continue to grow, it must provide perceived *value* for its participants, not only for marketers, but also for affiliates as well. The question is what are the scope and characteristics of this value, and which elements of affiliate marketing cause it. In examining this value, we look at the positive aspects as well as the negative, thus also covering the aspects that limit the attractiveness of affiliate marketing.

Which Considerations Should Firms go Through in Determining the Potential Use of Affiliate Marketing?

In determining if and how to adopt affiliate marketing, firms need to go through some process of evaluation, in order to understand strategic implications and possible options. This process should be based on their specific situation and needs, but there are undoubtedly some general elements of the evaluation process that are relevant for all firms, although presumably separate for marketers and affiliates respectively. We seek to identify what issues firms must address, including potential barriers that may limit or preclude the use of affiliate marketing for some firms.

The following chapters will deal with the issues confronting the different parties of affiliate networks in order to illuminate the important strategic and operational considerations to be dealt with.

1.6 OUTLINE OF THE BOOK

Chapter 2: Understanding Internet Customers

A solid understanding of customers is important for all firms, on the Internet as well as in the 'physical world'. This chapter provides a number of conceptions that can be used in that purpose. Even though some of the mechanisms of strategy and marketing might have changed, basic customer behaviour has not. The challenge is to find the bridge between traditional business virtues and the new logics of the Internet.

Chapter 3: What is Affiliate Marketing?

In this chapter, we perform a study of the roles and characteristics of each of three types of participant firms in an Affiliate network: marketers, affiliates and a broker. In this context, we examine the interactions with regards to forming and ending relationships, and the ongoing processes and transactions among the participants. The network is described in terms of six basic characteristics: structure, symmetry, continuity, interdependence, standardisation, and adaptation.

Chapter 4: Value Creation in Affiliate Marketing

Affiliate marketing is attractive to firms because of the value it provides for its participants. Eight key resources, each of which are created during the interactions between participants and/or exchanged among them, drive this value. These key resources are: brand, performance-based payments, technology platform, information, brokerage, context-based sales, consumer relations, and network relations. In practice, there are overlaps between the resources, but for explanatory and clarifying reasons we analyse each resource individually.

Chapter 5: Affiliate Considerations

With the perspective of the affiliate, affiliate marketing is considered at corporate, business, and operational level. In this view, affiliate marketing is analysed in regard to several potential benefits and drawbacks, among these are: the affiliates' commercial and editorial interests and conflicts, increased activity level, and budgeting considerations.

Chapter 6: Marketer Considerations

With the perspective of the marketer, affiliate marketing is considered at corporate, business, and operational levels. On corporate and business levels, the marketer's considerations are analysed with regard to resellers and channel conflicts, and control of marketing and brand activities. On the operational level we identify four set-ups of affiliate marketing, and evaluate each of them. They are: affiliate marketing as an alternative marketing channel; as a lead and sales generator; fully integrated to the marketers' back-end systems; and the reverse affiliate marketing model. The latter, allows for a set-up that involves the marketer's existing resellers.

Chapter 7: Explanation Model

In this chapter, we bring together Chapters 3–6 in a holistic perspective and focus on the links among them. We identify specific ties between the various roles, considerations and value elements firms can expect as part of an affiliate marketing network. Our basic assumption is that all four chapters are interrelated, meaning that what role a firm plays and how it fills out this role influences the value gained from affiliate marketing. We adopt the perspective of an affiliate and marketer respectively, and illustrate whether they gain value – positive or negative – from each of the value elements we identified in Chapter 4. We then indicate what types of roles affect these elements, and finally, how the value elements trigger strategic considerations.

1.7   KEY DEFINITIONS

Affiliate marketing occurs when two legally independent entities form a mutual agreement, where one party (the affiliate) communicates a message for the other (the marketer). The term refers to an online business relationship, where communication of a message to visitors at the affiliate's website can lead to possible transactions on the marketer's website. Due to tracking technology the transaction can be traced back to the affiliate, who is financially compensated after the transaction has occurred, based on predefined performance criteria.

An **affiliate marketing network** is the assortment of firms involved in affiliate marketing. The simplest affiliate marketing network consists of only one marketer and its affiliates. In this situation the affiliate signs up directly through the marketer, who is solely responsible for all administration and technical issues. However, in this book, we will focus only on the situation where an affiliate marketing provider acts as a broker between many possible marketers and many possible affiliates. The reason for this is mainly that a brokered network has many of the same characteristics as a single-marketer network, but also some additional characteristics. Furthermore, in studying a brokered solution, we can view several marketers at once, providing more diversity in our research. We provide a more specific explanation of the differences between single-marketer and brokered affiliate marketing in Chapter 3.

A **firm** describes a potential or current participant in an affiliate marketing programme. It is a separate decision-making entity. We use this terminology to cover the whole spectrum of participants. While some of these are personal or amateur websites, they participate in the programme to earn money, and we therefore refer to them all as 'firms'.

2. Understanding Internet Customers

As was stated in the previous chapter, the discourse on the new economy has been characterised by a strong technological imperative. A predominant part of the literature on e-business and e-commerce has taken its starting point in concepts like richness and reach and forgotten about traditional marketing virtues. We do however believe that even though we might experience a new economy today, we have to remember and honour some basic marketing virtues and strategic virtues.

In this chapter, we will discuss marketing on the Internet from the customers' point of view, in order to picture some basic functionalities before we introduce affiliate marketing as a strategic marketing option. It might be a blunt description but we can, in a marketing perspective, state that the Internet can be seen as a medium for communication and for transactions. In some cases, if your product is virtual, it can also be seen as a distribution channel. Put in other words, the Internet can be seen as a communications resource, a content resource and a channel resource (Coupey, 2001).

In this chapter we will go into the following areas, not so much with the purpose of accounting for normative statements for marketers, but rather with the purpose of understanding customers:

- Customer behaviour and purchasing patterns
- Product choice rationales and preferences
- Marketing communications.

Since this book is dealing primarily with affiliate marketing being a performance-based business model, we do not go into all different aspects of the marketing process. Marketing communications can, for example, have the aim of creating attention or a desire or an action. When discussing performance-based models not all these aims are in focus, but the actual transaction is laying the foundation for the relation in the affiliate network and the focus will hence be on the transactional dimensions of the above-stated areas.

2.1   CONSUMER BEHAVIOUR

In the early stages of e-commerce by means of the World Wide Web, the development was driven by utopian conceptions of the possibilities, such as: 'On the Internet, you can reach an infinite amount of consumers, who are all willing to buy anything on-line'. Arguments like convenience and price competition were brought forward as the main competitive dimensions taken into account. Another important issue is the decision process of consumers, where most spokesmen of e-commerce tended to view consumers as information seeking and rational in their decisions. The basic problem is that we cannot view all consumers as one homogeneous mass of individuals, all showing the same kind of consumer behaviour. A reason for this misconception might be some of the built-in arguments of the growth of Internet commerce. One major argument is that of market transparency, making it possible for consumers to make comparisons between offers in terms of product specifications and prices.

Since consumers try to maximise the benefit of consumption, whilst minimising the cost for consumption, this transparency of the Internet can lead to a perfect market. This argument is valid if and only if all consumers behave rationally like economic beings.

The Rational Consumer

There are many examples of models on consumer behaviour based on a rational decision process; one of these can be seen in Figure 2.1, where the central sequence is the actual decision process. It all starts out with need recognition, with the notion that this need can be satisfied by means of some kind of consumption of a product. The rational consumer then searches for alternatives and evaluates them. Based on this evaluation, a purchase is made leading to an outcome affected by perceptions of the consumption of the product in turn leading to either satisfaction or dissatisfaction.

The level of satisfaction will affect evaluation of alternatives the next time this consumer is going through the sequence. A high level of satisfaction will naturally lead to a favourable evaluation, whereas dissatisfaction will most likely lead to an external search for new alternatives. This external search is sometimes intentional, where the consumer actively seeks information, and sometimes influenced by external stimuli such as marketing communications. All results of external search mechanisms are stored in the individual's memory to be accessed when needed.

All parts of this process are affected by individual as well as environmental variables, showing that even if the rationality is the same, the process may differ from case to case, depending on these variables.

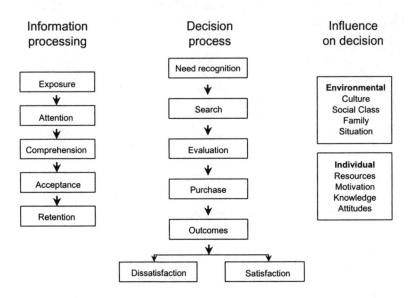

Source: Adapted from Engel et al., 1993

Figure 2.1   A model of consumer behaviour

Related to this rational decision process, there is also the way consumers are disposed towards certain products and concepts, and how they respond to stimuli regarding these products and concepts. If we believe in rational decisions, we also have to accept that a consumer goes through response hierarchies like those shown in Figure 2.2.

All these response hierarchies build on the conception of attitudes that is constituted by three components: the cognitive, the affective, and the conative (Fitzroy, 1976). A consumer's knowledge and recognition of a product is reflected by the cognitive component, the feelings for this product is reflected by the affective component, and finally the consumer's expressive inclination to act is reflected by the conative component. Thus, it is assumed that consumers go through a number of steps starting out with some kind of awareness of a product. This awareness is needed in order for someone to be interested and to desire the product, which in turn is necessary for action.

It might be unnecessary to state that all consumers do not behave in this rational manner, but might behave more irrationally in a lot of situations regarding their consumption. It is fairly easy to give spontaneous examples of situations where most consumers behave rationally or not as the case may be. As an example, when a consumer is going to buy an automobile or other durable consumer goods, the decision might be quite rational. On the other hand, when buying and consuming fast moving consumer goods, the process is less likely to be rational.

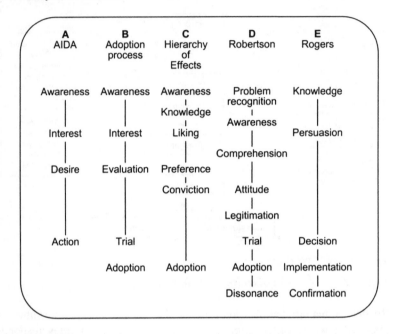

Figure 2.2. Different models for adoption processes

Product Differentiation

An alternative to the rational information processing hierarchies of effects is presented in the three-orders model of information processing (Ray, 1973), in Figure 2.3. Perceived product differentiation is stated to be an important dimension that can affect the way a consumer responds to communication or other stimuli.

The traditional learning response, where a consumer goes through the sequence of cognition, affection and action occurs when the perceived product differentiation is high and the topical involvement is high. The reason for this is that all the differences between products create an urge to evaluate alternatives, because the topical involvement is high. In the dissonance/attribute model there are no obvious differences in product attributes so the actual choice is not based on cognition or affection, but will develop ex post in order to support the decision. If all products, potentially satisfying this particular need, seem to be of the same quality and posses the same technical functionality, why should the consumer go through the process of cognition and affection before the decision?

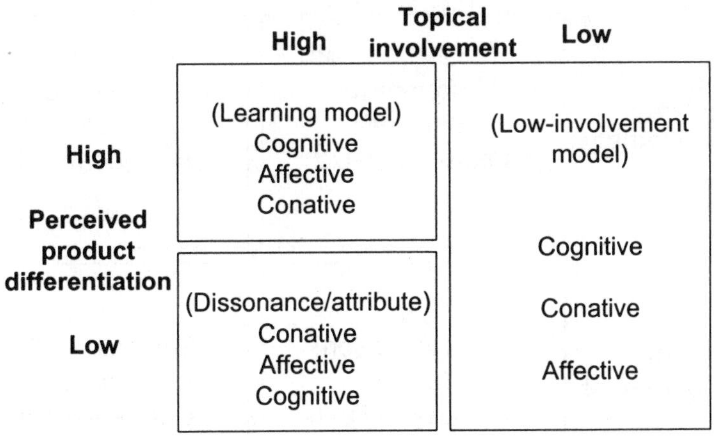

	Topical involvement	
	High	**Low**
High **Perceived product differentiation**	(Learning model) Cognitive Affective Conative	(Low-involvement model)
		Cognitive
Low	(Dissonance/attribute) Conative Affective Cognitive	Conative
		Affective

Source: Ray, 1973

Figure 2.3   Three-orders model of information processing

Ray is also discussing the concept of involvement, which has been stated to be of crucial importance for the kind of response that can be expected to stimuli in relation to specified objects or products.

Involvement

There is no single precise definition of involvement, but there is clearly a conception involving personal relevance, indicating that involvement is not general, but individual (Zaichkowsky, 1986). Involvement is affected by a number of variables, like individual characteristics, perceived risk, financial aspects, and the object as such. In Figure 2.4, an example of the importance of involvement is shown.

Vaughn is here introducing thinking and feeling processing as dimensions besides the level of involvement. Thinking means that a decision is made on reason and logic, *ethos*, and feeling on the contrary implies that the same decision can be made on emotions, *pathos*. With a high or low involvement, thinking and feeling, there is a resulting four-field matrix, showing different response hierarchies. The above-mentioned investment in an automobile would most likely be characterised as a situation of thinking and high involvement. Another example could be cosmetics or jewellery, where the

The basics of Internet marketing

consumer can be assumed to have a high involvement, but with feeling processing resulting in affective behaviour.

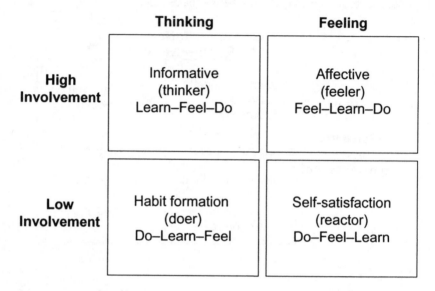

Source: Vaughn, 1980

Figure 2.4   The Foot, Cone and Belding (FCB) Grid

It is worth noticing that this model differs from the one shown in Figure 2.3, where there is only one model suggested for low involvement. According to Vaughn, low involvement leads to either do–feel–learn or to do–learn–feel, implying that there is nothing preceding action. Ray on the other hand argues that low involvement leads to learn–do–feel (cognitive–conative–affective), meaning that there has to be some cognitive aspects in place before a consumer acts, even in situations characterised by low involvement.

Is There a Model for Consumer Behaviour?

The discussion can so far be summarised as a brief one on what is driving consumption. In the traditional rational model, a cognitive conception of a problem is initiating a decision process eventually leading to a purchase and consumption of products. Put in other words, the initiating stimulus is internal. The other models presented build on a conception that consumers do not necessary go through that rational process, but might be more emotional or action-driven in their consumption patterns. In this case, the initiating stimulus is often external. One can always reflect on this discussion and ask oneself whether or not all consumption is in some way problem-driven. If consumers do not perceive a problem, why consume at all? This question cannot be answered without discussing the value of products. We often think of products satisfying needs and wants of consumers in terms of their technical functionality, but it is not always the case. Could it be so that a consumer sometimes just wants to shop, regardless of what is going to be bought? The gratification of a joyful shopping experience cannot be neglected even though the problem solved has nothing to do with the functionality of the product. Without going too deep into this discussion, we can conclude that consumption and purchase patterns can be driven by different factors from case to case. Regardless of the driving factor, there is still the issue of value. However illogical or emotional the buying and consumption situation might be, there is a perceived value involved, since the consumer has chosen to pay a certain amount of money for the product.

As a conclusion of this section, it can be stated that we cannot understand consumers' behavioural patterns, without a clear conception of the value that is provided by a certain product and vice versa. These different behavioural patterns pose challenges for marketing on the Internet as well as in the physical world. One of these challenges lies within communication with customers, which will be dealt with in the next section.

2.2   MARKETING COMMUNICATIONS

Marketing communications is a set of activities aiming to promote products, services and firms to a market. The communications mix consists of a number of activities like advertising, personal selling, public relations, sales promotion and direct marketing. We will not go into discussions on techniques for affiliate marketing in this section, since these will be dealt with in coming chapters, but look into some general foundations and virtues of marketing communications that have an impact on affiliate marketing.

The Communication Process

All communication involves sharing of information between two or more parties, where a key success factor is a common understanding of what is communicated. There can be many different purposes of intentional communication, but regardless of purpose, the basic communication process (Schram, 1955) can be described as in Figure 2.5.

The process starts out with a sender having an intention to communicate with a receiver in order to obtain a certain response. In the case of marketing communications, this response can for example, be attention or brand recognition, an increased level of desire or a higher inclination to buy a product. In order to make this happen, there are a number of critical decisions to be made. In the process of encoding, the sender must choose words, signs and symbols that make sense to the receiver. Through this encoding, a message is created, containing the information to be communicated. This message has to be transported in a suitable channel or vehicle, so that it reaches the right receiver. When the receiver is confronted with the message through this channel, the message is decoded, and hopefully interpreted in the way it was intended. Throughout this communicative process, the message is subject to external factors that can interrupt or distort the message. This unplanned distortion is labelled noise.

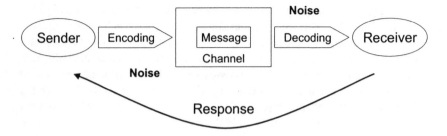

Source: Schram, 1955

Figure 2.5   A model of the communications process

Choice of Media

When creating a message and choosing a channel, the desired effect or response should be the first decision criterion. There is a significant difference in communicating a completely new product concept, trying to establish an understanding and a liking of the concept in comparison to stimulating sales in an established market. Successful communication is not just dependent upon the marketer and the customer, but also channel actors, or media as shown in Figure 2.6.

This exchange system of marketing communications involves three main actors; the advertiser, the consumer and the media. The fourth actor is the advertising agency providing the advertiser with supporting services. The central exchange process in this system is the transaction between the advertiser and the consumer. Without this transaction, the system will be redundant. Media do however play a very important role, since media function as channels for communication. The basic business logic for these media is to provide consumers with an attractive content, so that these consumers will be willing to 'pay' with their time. This exposure time can then be sold by the media, to advertisers, in the form of reach, frequency and impact (RFI). Reach is defined as the number of costumers exposed, frequency as the number of exposures, and impact as the effect the exposure has on customers. Advertisers can use these dimensions when evaluating media to be chosen.

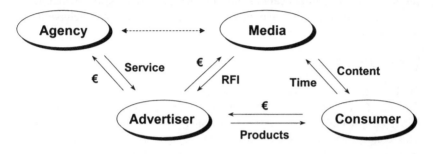

Figure 2.6   An exchange system in marketing communications

It should be recognised that this system is stereotypical in the sense that the roles and exchange processes are generic. Depending on contingencies, the boundaries between the roles might be blurred and the chain of events might be changing. In its generic mode, the system can be seen as an asynchronous exchange system, defining a sequence of events of communication and transactions. This is the case in, for example, traditional advertising, where a message is communicated in a selected medium in order to create a future response.

From the customers' point of view, it all has to make sense. If the desired effect or response is to occur, all parts have to be consistent. The message has to be encoded in an appropriate way and it has to be transported in an appropriate channel so that the customer can decode it the way it was intended. As an example, consider a firm selling a product with a 'life-style value' going beyond the technical functionality of the product in a market that is not price sensitive. In this case, the firm chooses to create a message that can help to strengthen the image of the product as being a life-style product. Even though the message in its style and form might be 'perfect', the right medium has to be chosen in order to establish the appropriate credibility. It has to make sense to the customer, to be exposed by a message communicating life-style values, in the selected medium. The challenge for the advertiser is then to find a medium providing a content that is interesting to this particular segment of the market, so that the right customers are exposed and the desired response will occur.

2.3   BUSINESS CUSTOMERS

The major difference between business-to-consumer (B2C) and business-to-business (B2B) marketing communications is that B2C communications are in most cases targeted towards consumers that will actually use the product or service. In B2B communications, the situation is more complex, which leads to a need for an understanding of demand structures and behaviour of business customers.

Derived Demand

Products in B2B markets are generally thought of as having a derived demand (Belch and Belch, 1995) meaning that the demand for products is derived from the need for other goods and services in consumer markets. This conception builds on the traditional value chain (Porter, 1980) where B2B products and services either can be parts of the value chain itself or function as supporting mechanisms.

A generalisation could state that without the derived demand of consumers, there would be no demand in B2B markets, since these firms are in business to serve other customers.

One can of course not take demand structures for granted, but one has to understand the particular market addressed and the demand structures of this market. Depending on these structures, there are different consequences for distribution, pricing and promotion of products and services (Gross et al., 1993). If a product is to be sold as a part of a value chain, with a derived demand, it might even be that in order to understand the B2B customers one has first to understand their customers or consumers.

Buying Behaviour

As for consumers, there are a number of factors in different levels affecting the buying process, such as environmental factors, organisational factors, buying centre factors and individual factors (Webster and Wind, 1972). We are not going into all these factors in this text, but will account for some issues we find important to address when discussing business customers and marketing on the Internet.

In most cases, in an organisational buying situation, there are a lot of individuals involved, which can be called the buying centre. These individuals, or actors, are more or less formally involved but will have an influence on the final outcome. The buying centre of a firm typically consists of the following actors:

- Initiators, who have authority to make the decision to make a purchase in the first place
- Users, who are going to actually use the product to be bought
- Influencers, who might have an informal influence on the decision
- Deciders, who have the authority to make the actual purchase decision
- Buyers, who are responsible for the transaction
- Gatekeepers, who are in control of the flow of information into and out of the organisation.

The individuals involved in the buying centre will collectively form a cognitive mindset influencing buying behaviour. This formation of a mindset is not an intentional process, but a consequence of subconscious mental processes. Depending on this mindset, buying behaviour can be distinctively different from situation to situation.

Another important issue is the kind of buying process in question. There is a difference in behaviour if it is the case of a new task, a straight re-buy or a modified re-buy. The mix of marketing activities will have a different nature in different situations and the importance of different actors in the buying centre will be different. A comparison between the two extremes: a straight re-buy and a new task, shows that a new task situation will most likely involve more people and more search for external information than a straight re-buy.

Problem-solving as Value

As was stated in the introductory chapter, the reason-to-be for all firms is to provide a value to a market eventually leading to transactions and interactions between parties in the market. In consumer markets this value might not always be related to the technical quality of the product as such but is sometimes related to more emotional aspects of consumption. Furthermore, consumer markets tend to be characterised by many small and rather passive buyers with not much dependence of suppliers. B2B markets do not comply with these characteristics, since buyers are larger and active due to the nature of their needs. There is a complex interdependence between buyer and supplier since the problems to be solved are often complex.

Håkansson (1980) uses the concept of 'problem-solving ability' in order to describe the capabilities of a supplier to meet the needs of their customers. This ability can be developed at different levels and can be of a general or adaptive nature. A high general ability means that a supplier can solve problems of customers as a group, and a high adaptive ability means that a supplier can individualise the problem solution to meet particular needs.

Combinations of these two abilities and marketing strategies are summarised in Figure 2.7.

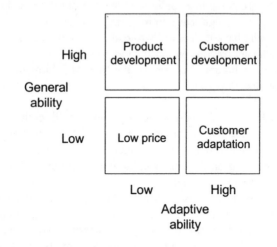

Source: Håkansson, 1980

Figure 2.7   Marketing strategies related to problem-solving abilities

The low price strategy builds on a basic assumption that there are no specific demands on technical quality or any commonalities between different customers. A completely standardised product can meet these demands and therefore the competitive strength of the supplier lies within cost reduction. The customer adaptation strategy builds on the customers' demand for a product fully adapted to the specific problem of that particular customer. There are no specific requirements of highly sophisticated technical solutions in a general sense, so the competitive strength mainly depends on the flexibility of the supplier. The product development strategy is based on customers who put a great emphasis on the functional qualities of the product but without any specific requirements on adaptation to specific needs. In order to be competitive, suppliers have to have an extensive knowledge of the general needs of customers and good skills in product development. The customer development strategy could be seen as a combination of customer adaptation and product development. In this case the demand of customers is of a complex nature, involving both specialisation and flexibility. Interactions in this kind of situation often tend to take the form of joint-venture development projects and do in most cases lead to long relationships for co-operation between supplier and buyer.

The problem-solving abilities are important when adopting an inside-out strategic perspective, and it is equally important to understand how business customers relate to information technology solutions. A significant number of firms in the focus of affiliate marketing networks are small and medium-sized firms, SMEs. Among SMEs, there are three important strategic dispositions to information technology (Junghagen, 1998, 1999):

- A proactive disposition, with a high level of perceived dynamics and inclination for change. The driving force for this inclination is internal and information technology is seen as a tool for strategic development.
- A reactive disposition, still with a high level of perceived dynamics and inclination to change, but with a driving force for change mainly induced by external factors in the environment. Information technology is seen as a tool for adaptive change.
- An inactive disposition, with a low level of perceived dynamics and without a strong inclination for change and development. In this case, information technology is seen as a means to achieve structural stability.

The question is then, what kind of firms show these kinds of strategic dispositions. There are five typical clusters of firms that can be viewed as general segments in the SME B2B market (ibid.):

- Industrial bureaucracies, i.e. relatively large firms with a high degree of formalisation and standardisation. Information technology is used to a large extent, but in an inactive way. Managers are not striving for change and development of the firm. The main motive for using information technology is a structural influence, external as well as internal. These structures are also rather stable.
- Sustenance firms, i.e. relatively small firms, with a high degree of formalisation and standardisation. Information technology is used to a low degree and if it is used, it is in an inactive way. There are a lot of similarities between this group and the industrial bureaucracies, except for the size of the firm. Motives for using information technology are the same, namely a structural influence characterised by stability.
- Professional service firms, i.e. small firms with extremely entrepreneurial managers and a high level of information technology use. The firms in this group are mostly within the professional service sector, e.g. marketing consultants, software consultants and other knowledge-intensive services. Information technology is perceived as a natural component of the firm's core competencies and is mainly used in a proactive way to support high dynamics.
- Local growth firms, i.e. small firms that are rapidly growing and dynamic. Information technology is not used to any wider extent and entrepreneurial tendencies among managers are not especially

significant, with an exception of an inclination for change. The customer base is mostly local with a high level of customer complexity. It seems that overall strategies as well as the use of information technology are mainly formed in a reactive and adaptive mode.

- Industrial adhocracies, i.e. generally relatively large firms, with a sophisticated use of information technology in a reactive way and a high level of information intensity. There is a low level of standardisation and formalisation among these firms. Decision-making is very much decentralised. Managers in this group are characterised by a high inclination for change, as well as competitive edge.

The implication of these strategic dispositions and the different segments of the market is that even though we can state that information-technology-based solutions have a strategic importance for customers, we cannot immediately tell how. If a problem-solving ability involves information technology as a supporting infrastructure, it is important to understand that not all customers have the disposition to see this ability, since their disposition might not be compatible with the intended ability.

It all comes down to the generic strategic direction of the customer, since their perception of any given problem solution will be affected by their perception of their strategic landscape.

2.4　THE INTERNET AND THE USERS

It should be obvious that we advocate a concept that we cannot sell anything to anyone on the Internet. First of all, one needs a clear understanding of the perceived value of the offer. Second, an understanding of what kind of information and decision process the consumer goes through. By means of these, one can determine what kind of marketing efforts that should be pursued. Before we go into the field of affiliate marketing, we should also have a look at some general tendencies in the use of the Internet. The findings presented here are extracted from reports of the World Internet Project, a global research project involving comparative studies on Internet user patterns and behaviour.

There are three main questions we will point out here. First of all, how do users spend their time on the Internet? We know that there is a huge mass of Internet users, but how do these users spend their time when they are online? Secondly, what are the barriers against electronic commerce? Since they are online, but do not spend so much time on shopping, what are the reasons for this? Third, the users that actually do shop on the Internet, how do they access retailers on the Internet?

The answers to these questions, accounted for below, are of course on an aggregated level, not showing interrelations between different findings, but do still give an overview of these tendencies.

How do Users Spend Their Time on the Internet?

An important issue, when assessing the potential market size on the Internet, is understanding how people spend their time when they are online. It cannot be taken for granted that Internet access automatically leads to an inclination to use the Internet for shopping. According to results from the World Internet Project, as can be seen in Figure 2.8, US users spend approximately 4 per cent of their time on the Internet for shopping.

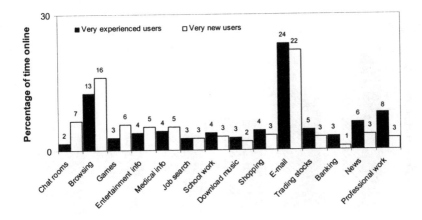

Source: UCLA, 2001

Figure 2.8   Relative distribution of activities on the Internet among USA users

It seems that there is an experience effect, since more experienced users tend to spend more relative time for shopping than new users. Most of the time is spent on checking e-mail and general browsing. There are differences between new users and more experienced users, but there are fairly clear tendencies that shopping is not an activity taking too much time of the users' online presence.

This does not necessarily imply an important problem for marketers on the Internet, since these are relative figures. The total amount of time spent on shopping might still be on a satisfactory level. The question is how this situation can be changed, so that more time is spent on shopping in the future.

We will now account for some general barriers against electronic commerce in order to understand that.

Barriers Against E-Commerce

If we now picture a typical consumer with an Internet access, showing the inclination to buy a certain product, what are the reasons for this potential consumer not to buy it on the Internet?

As seen in Figure 2.9, the most important reason is a fear of credit card fraud. Internet users are typically concerned with giving up information on their credit card details, since there might be a risk of violation of their card. There are secure systems available, but there is still a negative disposition among users.

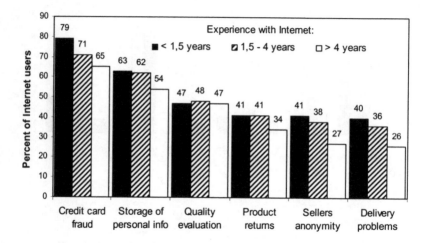

Source: Findahl, 2001

Figure 2.9   Concern over problems with Internet shopping among Swedish users

Another important issue is the storage of personal information. Most consumers are not that enthusiastic about giving personal information, just because they are buying a product. If the choice is between giving information or not to buy, they choose not to buy. The other dimensions shown in Figure 2.9 can all be seen as related to the delivery system as such. It is hard to evaluate product quality, there is a concern over problems with product returns, sometimes the seller is anonymous and the delivery of products is not always as good as it should be.

Among those who actually shop on the Internet, the final question is then how they access the retailers.

Access to Retailers

A European research study by the Boston Consulting Group (2000a) showed how customers access an online retailer's website/store. Of total traffic to these sites, 7 per cent and 10 per cent were referred through affiliates for multichannel retailers and pure-play online retailers respectively.

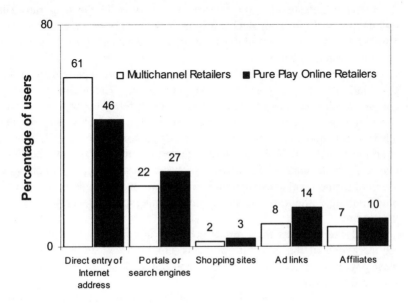

Source: BCG, 2000a

Figure 2.10   How customers access online retailers

Even though access through affiliates seems to be low in relation to other access modes, one should keep in mind that access as such does not generate sales. As many Internet users search for information online before purchasing offline (Strauss and Frost, 1999) it is hard to keep track of results by just tracking access. As will be shown in the following chapters, this is handled through affiliate programmes, where objectives are matched with desired performance of the affiliates.

2.5 CHAPTER CONCLUSION

As has been argued in this chapter, taking behaviour of customers into account does not make marketing on the Internet an easy task. A spontaneous question might be how one ever can determine appropriate marketing action, when prerequisites for these actions seem to be so contingent. However, even though decisions have to be contingency dependent, there are some general remarks that can be made in order to relate to customers on the Internet.

First of all, there is the issue of value propositions. Without creating value for someone outside the firm, no firm will survive in the long run. This statement is valid for both B2C and B2B markets. Therefore, any marketing effort should take its point of departure in an understanding of the perceived value the firm is offering.

Second, the marketer needs to understand consumption patterns regarding this kind of value proposition among consumers. The above section on consumer behaviour has brought forward some different conceptions of what is driving consumption. Some models argue for the rational consumer whilst others claim that more emotional forces drive consumption. It is not our intention to tell which one of these arguments is the correct one, but leave that to the reflections of the reader. The basic question to put though, when discussing emotional consumption, is whether a consumer can be expected to buy anything without having any cognitive understanding whatsoever about the product.

Third, the marketer must reflect upon the appropriateness of the Internet for marketing of the particular products and services. Shopping is not the most popular activity on the Internet, and not all kinds of products can be sold on the Internet.

When a marketer is deciding on creating or joining an affiliate network, there are a number of issues to deal with. The above discussion on consumer behaviour and marketing communications illuminates some of the problems at hand. It is a matter of understanding what kind of communication objective makes sense in relation to the target market in order to define expected performance by the affiliate. The choice of affiliates is also dependent on the target market and its relation to the affiliates. The blurring of boundaries between the elements in the marketing mix, mentioned in Chapter 1, makes it even more complicated. Should the affiliate be treated as a communication channel, or a sales channel, or both? These issues will be fully covered in Parts II and III.

PART II

What is Affiliate Marketing?

What is Affiliate Marketing?

Affiliates and marketers are interdependent, because one's content serves as input for the other. Therefore, in order to gain value in an affiliate marketing network, participants stand strong when they understand the concepts and principles that are evident for all parties involved. In Chapter 3, we clarify the principles of affiliate marketing by examining firms' purposes of joining an affiliate network, how transactions are defined between the parties, the payment structure, and how affiliate marketing evolved from a one-to-one relationship to a one-to-many relationship. Eventually the principles of affiliate marketing became applicable to an increasing number of online businesses, creating the foundation for a separate industry of affiliate marketing where many marketers interact with many affiliates via a third party facilitator, the broker.

In explaining the implication of an affiliate marketing network, from the perspective of each participant, we view the network on three levels: (1) the individual organisations, (2) inter-organisational relationships, and (3) the network.

The forming of relations in affiliate marketing typically takes place 'bottom-up', in which affiliates apply to the marketer's programme, based on the general conditions set forward by the marketer. Hereafter, the marketer can accept or reject the application. To make these relationships worthwhile for the marketer, and to take advantage of economies of scale in the network the relationships need to be standardised, so that they demand very few resources. For this reason, marketer–affiliate relationships are standardised via the technology platform. The interdependence between marketers and affiliates often increases over time, as they adapt their content and the general conditions to each other to increase the overall effectiveness of their relationship. For this reason, affiliate marketing appears to engender long-term relationships.

Participants' reasons for joining an affiliate marketing network are evidently to gain value from being connected to many other resources and benefit from the network effect and ultimately to create increased value for themselves. In Chapter 4 we analyse how potential value is achieved, and the potential risks involved.

Based on the principles and implications of affiliate marketing and through exploratory interviews with marketers, affiliates, media agencies, and employees at TradeDoubler, we identified eight key resources that are established in the interaction between the participants. Each of the key resources is analysed, in turn, on how to create value for each of the participants. The key resources are: brand, performance-based payment, technology platform, information, brokerage, context-based sales, end-user relations, and network relations.

3. Affiliate Marketing Networks

We commence this chapter by outlining the basic principles of affiliate marketing, followed by a brief discussion of a brokered vs. an in-house affiliate marketing solution. Building on this, we continue by analysing in greater depth the participants, their interactions, and the characteristics of an affiliate marketing network.

3.1 BASIC PRINCIPLES OF AFFILIATE MARKETING

Affiliate marketing is an agreement where one firm (the marketer) compensates another firm (the affiliate) for generating transactions from its users (Maloney, 2001). In practice, it involves a marketer placing links to its website on affiliated websites. These links can be in the form of text, product pictures or other images that aim to promote a message to potential customers. Rather than pay for these links up front, the marketer provides a commission to affiliates for every transaction that results from these links. When a user clicks on a link at an affiliate's website, he is transferred to the marketer's website, where he can take further action. A software tool tracks (measures) the user's path and notes the affiliate website that made the referral so that the marketer can pay the affiliate a predetermined commission fee (IDC, 1999). Hence the payment is performance-based, as affiliates are paid only for the transactions they generate, rather than on the number of advertising impressions they show. If organised correctly, it can potentially benefit both parties, because it helps marketers acquire new customers and increase revenues, while affiliates can generate revenue from the visitors to their websites (Maloney, 2001).

The transaction that an affiliate gets compensated for can take three main forms, depending on what marketer and affiliate agree upon when forming the relationship. The first is *sales*, where affiliates can receive a percentage of the sales generated by users referred from the affiliate. Commissions on sales can range from 5 per cent to 25 per cent of the sale price (IDC, 1999), depending on the profit margins of the products sold. Second, affiliates can be compensated for generating *leads*, which entail that the visitors they refer submit information to the marketer that it can follow up on. The marketer will typically request this information, such as when a customer signs up for a membership, or subscribes to a newsletter. Commissions on leads are usually at flat rates. This fee can vary substantially, depending on the type of business the marketer has and thus the value of a potential customer. Finally, affiliates can get compensated for clicks, where their visitors simply click on the marketer's link and are transferred to the marketer's website, without further action required from the visitor. Commission on clicks is always a flat fee. The commission structure can vary from marketer to marketer, and will often be based on a combination of the aforementioned transaction types (Helmstetter and Metivier, 2000).

The purpose of affiliate marketing is not just awareness building, since affiliates are typically not paid for showing marketing messages (impressions), but for transactions where the user actively responds. This differs from impression-based advertising, of which banner ads are the most widespread online (IDC, 1999). Hence, the different software associated with affiliate marketing and banner ads measure different things, since the objectives and payment structure are different. Figure 3.1 illustrates whether each of the two marketing techniques measures the various types of transactions, including impressions.

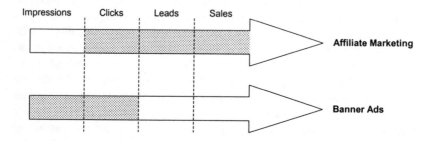

Figure 3.1   Tracking differences between banner ads and affiliate marketing

It is possible to track impressions with affiliate marketing technology, but this is not what the marketer pays for. Even if the full tracking technology was available to both affiliate marketing brokers and banner networks the business models are different, and marketers use the two models for different advertisement purposes. It should be noted that whether the two methods actually measure the different types of transactions depends to some degree on how these transaction types are defined. We define an affiliate marketing transaction as: 'an economically motivated exchange of products and services, in which the end-user, marketer and affiliate are involved'. This definition implies that we want to register when the end-user interacts with the marketer through the affiliate. In further operationalising it, we define transactions according to the four possible ways in which sales and/or marketing can take place in an interaction where all three parties are involved *through use of the World Wide Web*: (1) impression, (2) click, (3) lead, and (4) sale. We characterise a specific transaction according to the 'highest' category that defines it.

An impression occurs when an end-user is exposed to some form of marketing message from a marketer through a website/affiliate. Operationally, we define it as a hyperlink to the marketer's website on a web page that an end-user (client) requests. The hyperlink can be 'anchored' into text or images. An impression is not registered as part of an affiliate's performance in our definition of affiliate marketing.

A click occurs when an end-user actively responds to a marketer's message. Operationally, we define it as occurring when the end-user activates the hyperlink in an impression, thus being transferred to its destination. Furthermore, it can also be defined in terms of a unique visitor. Unique visitors are registered once per a defined time period. TradeDoubler uses the operational definition of a click as being a unique visitor per each 24 hours.

A lead is an action performed by the end-user on the marketer's site that is registered in the marketer's affiliate programme, and which the marketer can follow up on in the future. Operationally, we define it as when an end-user submits data about him or herself on request from the marketer.

A sale is when the end-user confirms an order on the marketer's site. Operationally, we define it as the transferral of money from the end-user to the marketer (not before), in return for the goods ordered within 14 days after the end-user transfers through a hyperlink from the affiliate to the marketer.

The user gets exposed to a product or a service in the context of the environment he or she is in, when using the Internet, and the marketer pays the affiliate based on predefined performance criteria. A more elaborate description of the differences between an in-house affiliate marketing programme and a brokered solution is presented below. In the USA, there are several brokers that run affiliate marketing programmes for marketers, and in Europe there are a few, of which one, TradeDoubler, is the largest.

3.2 IN-HOUSE VS. BROKERED AFFILIATE MARKETING

The simplest affiliate marketing network consists of only one marketer and its affiliates. Affiliates signs up directly through the marketer, who is solely responsible for all administration and technical issues. There are more than one thousand of these types of programmes (Silverstein, 2001), of which Amazon.com's is the largest with more than 400,000 affiliates (Bruner et al., 2001). However, due to the amount of administration in terms of support, segmentation, and payments to many thousands of affiliates as well as the need for a continuous technological development, many marketers outsource their affiliate marketing needs to specialised 'brokers' that handle programmes for many marketers (IDC, 1999). Their services include maintaining the technology platform and administering payments, as well as recruiting affiliates. Nonetheless, the principles of the business models are somewhat similar. End-users get exposed to a product or a service in the context of the environment they are in when using the Internet, and marketers pay affiliates based on predefined performance criteria. While in this book we only focus on the situation where an affiliate marketing provider acts as a broker between many possible marketers and many possible affiliates, it is important to note the differences between the two types of affiliate marketing networks, in order to understand the viability of affiliate marketing in a larger perspective.

According to TradeDoubler, in addition to the economies of scale in administration and technology development, the two major differences between an in-house and a brokered solution are that in the latter there is (1) more of a network effect, and (2) a specific 'broker' function. For example, Amazon.com's associate programme is an in-house solution with one marketer maintaining relationships with many affiliates. A brokered solution can in principle also provide such a set-up for a single marketer, but the relationships in a brokered affiliate network are typically characterised by 'many (marketers)-to-many (affiliates)'. TradeDoubler's affiliate marketing network has its point of origin in a brokered version with relationships that are characterised as being many-to-many.

With regard to the network effect, the in-house solution offers a one-to-many relationship, where the marketer has full control over the affiliate network, but affiliates only have a single marketer to partner with. On the other hand, in the brokered solution many marketers can share the same affiliate network, and affiliates can refer to more than one marketer. An affiliate could, for example, refer to both a bookstore and a computer store, perhaps creating more relevant links for its users than a single marketer could provide. This is illustrated in Figure 3.2.

The broker's function is that of an independent third party between the affiliate website and the marketer website, securing stability in the relationship by tracking traffic and handling payments to affiliates in accordance with users' behaviour.

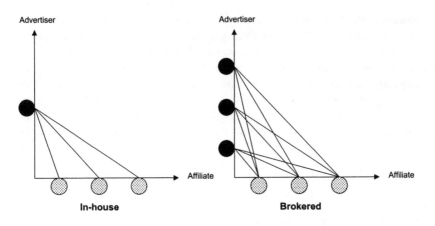

Figure 3.2   An affiliate marketing network as in-house and brokered solutions.

There are many variations of the broker's function in the network, for example brokers don't handle commission payments for marketers. However, our case is based on the business model of the biggest affiliate marketing broker in Europe – TradeDoubler – that does handle this function. As already mentioned, in a brokered affiliate network, the broker handles development of the technical platform, tracking capabilities, and maintenance for the benefit of the entire network. These considerations can be of great value for merchants who don't have the technical skills and resources in-house to maintain their affiliate programme, which can be very costly.

3.3   THE AFFILIATE MARKETING NETWORK

In the subsequent part of this chapter, we examine how affiliate marketing is carried out in practice through an analysis of the participating firms and their interactions. Our empirical object is TradeDoubler's European affiliate marketing network. The network consists of over 400,000 firms, of which there is one broker (TradeDoubler) and about 500 marketers, with the remainder being affiliates. And we view the network on three levels: (1) the individual organisations, (2) inter-organisational relationships, and (3) the network.

We start by analysing the characteristics and roles of the participating organisations. We look at each of the three distinct roles in the network: marketers, affiliates and the broker. After that, we move on to studying the interactions that take place in the network. We view them as taking place through inter-organisational relationships among individual marketers and affiliates, facilitated by the broker. We examine the forming and ending of relations, as well as the ongoing processes. Finally, we shift focus to the level of the entire network. Here we examine the characteristics of the network according to a selection of categories developed by Alexander (1995), Hall (1996), and Håkansson and Snehota (1995). We rest on the argument posed by these authors that a network must be seen holistically in order to capture some important insights that cannot be grasped on the level of its individual parts.

3.4   PARTICIPANTS

According to Hall (1996): 'the roles organisations play relative to one another, in terms of their programmes and services and clients to be served, are critical issues for the organisations involved'. It may be noted that some firms can have multiple roles in the network, for example, a few firms are both marketers and affiliates. The broker can also serve as a marketer (it recruits new affiliates through affiliates). This does not impact our analysis significantly, as these multiple roles can be viewed as separate. The partnerships they form in each role are not contingent on their other roles. However, firms that are active as both affiliates and merchants are assumed to be better positioned to understand the mechanisms of an affiliate network, as the merchants and the affiliates are interdependent and benefit from each other's resources.

Marketers' Characteristics

Marketers are firms that seek to reach an interest group online, mainly customers to whom they can sell products and/or services. These customers can be consumers and/or businesses. They participate in an affiliate marketing programme in order to enlist affiliates to help them reach potential customers or other interest groups that affiliates come into contact with. Other than this, there are few limitations to the characteristics a marketer must have.

In the network we examined, there are more than 500 marketers (in Europe). They typically belong to one of two categories, either large Internet-based companies or fairly large traditional companies with a strong Internet presence. The reason for this is that TradeDoubler must be discriminating in which marketers they invite into the network. Many relationships are rapidly established between marketers and affiliates, and the affiliates become dependant on the stability of the marketer to deliver goods and services, commissions for generated clicks, leads and sales, creative material etc.

Some products and services are better than others at selling through an affiliate marketing programme. A few key criteria seem to have an influence of the suitability of a certain type of product or service. First and foremost, the product should be relatively easy to communicate through the Internet, which as a media has its own characteristics. This is evident in a study of the first products that were successfully marketed and achieved online sales volume. In 1997, products that represented the top online spending were PCs (20 per cent), travel (16 per cent), software (13 per cent), books (8 per cent), flowers and gifts (3 per cent) and music (2 per cent) (Strauss and Frost, 1999). Other products expected to increase in the future are clothing, cars, and consumer electronics. These products and services generally have some attributes that make them attractive for online sales (adapted from Strauss and Frost, 1999):

- Non-perishable – The items can be shipped without spoiling, or can be transferred electronically.
- High relative value – The items are often relatively expensive and high-involvement.
- Information intensive – The items require research to be done before purchasing.
- High-tech – A high percentage of Internet users are technology-interested, especially the heavy users most likely to purchase online.

While there are exceptions to every rule, products with some or all of these characteristics are more likely to be purchased online. Naturally, affiliates select the marketers they want to work with based on what they think they will gain the most from. For example, according to research firm IDC (1999), marketers selling high-ticket items such as cars or jewellery attract fewer affiliates than marketers selling books or clothes, because affiliates find it easier to sell the latter. However, affiliate marketing is more than selling products, it is also about generating leads for future sales or contacts. Therefore, some companies that not only sell products, but also want to recruit employees or generate leads to follow up offline, are also involved in affiliate marketing.

The Marketers' Role

The Marketers' role in the network is to provide the content (information, products, services) that consumers find attractive. Since affiliate marketing is founded on performance-based payment, it is critical to affiliates that consumers are enticed to go directly from their site to a marketer's site and perform a transaction (e.g. make a purchase or registration). It is also a big asset if marketers have an apparatus to follow up on potential customers through call centres or e-mail. A good customer relationship management system can go a long way in this regard.

To optimise sales, marketers should provide affiliates with creative material that illustrates their offers. Typically, marketers have a section on the broker's website where they can place creative links of products and prices, along with special images and logos. Affiliates can go to the website and copy any link or image they want to their own website. All images are linked to their relevant web page on the marketer's website, so that users that click on them will be directly transferred. It is also important that marketers maintain a simple website that makes it easy for consumers to navigate. User tests of Internet sites show that one of the major irritations for consumers is that they find it difficult to actually complete a purchase on many websites. According to a Boston Consulting Group study of 12,000 consumers, 28 per cent of all attempted purchases fail, most often due to technical problems or problems finding the desired products (Lindstrom, 2001). Optimally, visitors clicking on an offer at an affiliate site should go directly to the purchasing page at the marketer (if purchase is the marketer's success criterion), or if needed a page with product information.

Also important to the success of the network is that marketers formulate well-defined performance criteria according to which affiliates are paid. Since the affiliate marketing network is founded on performance-based payment, marketers have to define the performance criteria. A purchase is defined as a completed sale generated through the affiliate. In this case the affiliate is paid a percentage of these revenues or a flat fee. Leads are defined differently for each marketer, for example the affiliate is paid for each registration, subscription to newsletters, or another explicitly defined user-session performed by a potential consumer. In general, TradeDoubler has defined a click as a unique visitor per 24 hours. This definition is made to avoid misuse and fraud; for example, to avoid the situation where an affiliate could build software that constantly generates clicks-through to a marketer's site, just to earn commissions. TradeDoubler assists marketers in setting the success criteria, based on their previous experience, but ultimately marketers must decide what they want to achieve from their affiliates, and what they are willing to pay them for it.

When the success criteria are defined in line with the marketer's online strategy, the marketer offers a payment structure that affiliates can choose to accept. However, if marketers set the payments too low, they may not get affiliates to join and stay long enough to build long-term relationships. It is critical to build long-term stability and success in the relations between marketers and affiliates in order to create a win/win situation. Hence, it is essential that the marketer can be flexible and differentiate commissions to different affiliates, depending on their performance.

Affiliates' Characteristics

Firms or private people that have a website can sign up as an affiliate at TradeDoubler. Beyond that, the only screening criterion by TradeDoubler is whether the affiliate is deemed 'unethical', i.e. regarded as being pornographic, violent or racist. Naturally this leaves room for interpretation, the common criterion used in screening potential affiliates was that they could have limited nudity on their site, but no overt sex or strongly sexually suggestive pictures.

In the TradeDoubler network there are about 400,000 affiliates, or approximately 1,000 for every marketer. In general, the affiliates in TradeDoubler's network are very varied in most aspects. They range in size from small hobby sites with practically no visitors to large traditional media companies with thousands of visitors a day.

According to TradeDoubler, it is important to segment affiliates into different categories, because there is such a difference among affiliates (see Figure 3.3). It initially splits affiliates into three main categories, based on their size/traffic and their level of specialisation/focus. The three categories are:

1. Hobby sites. These are affiliates with relatively low traffic. This group makes up about 75 per cent of all affiliates.
2. Vertical sites. These are affiliates that have chosen to specialise in a certain topic. They typically have medium traffic, and with a very focused audience. They make up about 20 per cent of affiliates.
3. Super Affiliates. These affiliates are the mass media websites that draw a large amount of traffic, but are relatively unfocused in their content and audience. They make up about 5 per cent of affiliates.

Private people maintaining the websites out of a non-professional interest or for a club typically run the hobby sites. These are defined as having 0–10,000 visitors per month. Twenty per cent of them typically move into the next segment, the vertical sites, as they develop over time. Vertical sites are characterised as both private people and businesses developing a website out of certain niche interests. They often have loyal visitors that visit the site on a regular basis and are defined as having 10,000–50,000 visitors per month. Twenty per cent of them typically move into the next segment, Super Affiliates, as they develop over time. The Super Affiliates are characterised as businesses and organisations that evaluate the revenue potential of affiliate marketing in comparison with banner advertisement and other business opportunities. They usually have daily updates of the website, less loyal visitors, and more than 50,000 visitors a month.

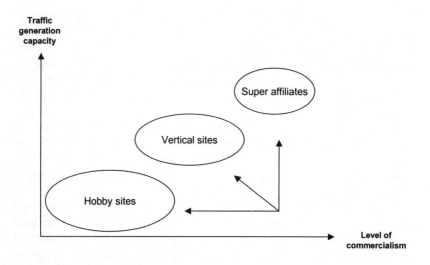

Figure 3.3   Segmentation on traffic capacity and commercialism

Marketers usually have to pay a higher click commission to Super Affiliates than to the two other categories. This is mainly due to the fact that they have a higher bargaining power. Also, the mass media are less focused and the incentive to buy via them is reduced relative to vertical sites, thus, the Super Affiliates are usually less interested in sales commissions than click commissions.

Affiliate's Role

The affiliate's role in an affiliate marketing network is to provide quality traffic, i.e. a steady flow of consumers willing to purchase products and services or to register themselves with marketers for further contact. It is not necessary that an affiliate's visitors represent a broad audience, on the contrary, it is often more effective when affiliates have a very targeted and specialised audience. If each of several thousand affiliates has a targeted audience, they can add up to form a broad range of visitors. A traditional example is a bookstore that sells a very broad range of books through its affiliates, many of which are small, specialised hobby sites.

It is important that affiliates' communities correspond to marketers' target groups. It would not be very productive for a website targeted towards children to link to a business-oriented site, since the marketer has a totally different target group. Although there may be some sales, the affiliate would probably do a lot better by marketing a more relevant product. The strength of affiliate marketing, according to both many affiliates and marketers, is that this selection is first and foremost the responsibility of affiliates. While marketers do care about which websites they are associated with, for affiliates it can be a matter of survival that they generate revenue, so they will usually spend some time in making sure that they choose marketers that have relevance for their communities. Since there are many times as many affiliates as marketers, we refer to this phenomenon as bottom-up formation of relationships. Rather than a few large marketers deciding where to advertise, the decision-making is effectively decentralised to many smaller units. Nevertheless, there must be a mutual acceptance between the marketer and the affiliate before a relationship is established.

Affiliates draw traffic by maintaining some type of content that visitors seek out. For Super Affiliates, this content is usually in the form of news, entertainment, articles and the like. For vertical websites, it is usually specialised articles and information on an in-depth subject. For hobby sites, it is usually personal information supplemented with some type of specialised information. Affiliates should keep their content up to date, although this is more important obviously for some types of content (e.g. news) than others. More than just providing content, productivity in affiliate marketing is increased dramatically if users develop a 'relationship' with affiliates. This is very difficult to quantify, but particularly focused sites can build quite a strong following among their visitors, sometimes described as a 'community' (Armstrong and Hagel, 1996; Hagel and Armstrong, 1997; Levine et al., 2000). Visitors actually trust the information of the site, especially when the authors express their own opinions. Sometimes the authors are the users, at least on some parts of the website (Armstrong and Hagel, 1996). It is usually easy for most consumers to trust news stories from large news agencies or media companies, but to trust specialised information about strongly personal and 'subjective' areas requires a relationship with the source and/or author (Levine et al., 2000).

Affiliates that have built this type of relationship with their visitors appear to perform much better in affiliate marketing than those that have not. For example, when a web editor people respect recommends a book as a good supplement to his articles, sales increase substantially. As long as he clearly notes that he makes commission by selling the book, but that this does not take away from the value of the book to users, affiliates believe their credibility is still intact. This is how Amazon.com's affiliate marketing programme, which was based on book reviews from small hobby websites, started (Kjærsdam, 2000). At the same time, some of the credibility is transferred to the marketer and its products. A recommendation by a trusted source can be seen as a quality stamp on the product, and even on the marketer (Levine et al., 2000). Marketers desperately want these types of endorsements, as they are seen as a type of 'controlled word of mouth'. This term is somewhat of an oxymoron, because typically it isn't word of mouth if you control it, but marketers only to a limited degree control the actual wording of the recommendation, by the rewards and the material made available to the sender (affiliate). Having thousands of specialised experts strongly recommending their products is every marketer's dream. But this vision is part of an ideal vision of the 'pure' affiliate marketing concept. As we show later, this vision is often unattainable due to various barriers in the marketplace. In any case, there is also an ethical dilemma associated with this type of marketing, and we get into that later on.

Another important role for affiliates is to know their audience. They should be able to not only choose a marketer with a good match, but also be able to choose the products and services that are most attractive to their audience, and place them correctly around their site. Since web users typically learn to skim web pages and move around quickly, small adjustments in placements of images in relation to content can have a big difference (Bruner et al., 2001). Affiliates should be able to provide this information to marketers to help them make offers that are more attractive to their audiences. There are currently no processes for affiliates to share this type of information with marketers. However, it is possible for the marketer to track performance of each individual link on the affiliate's site, thus gaining its own information.

Brokers' Characteristics

A broker is the firm that maintains the affiliate marketing programme/platform. The company does not necessarily need to be solely Internet-based, as the programme software can be bought or leased from a software company. In fact, a French and US-based company, i-mediation, does lease software specifically to companies wanting to run an affiliate marketing programme. While this software was meant mainly for large marketers wanting to run their own propriety programme, several smaller brokers use it as well. A number of media agencies also lease software and offer affiliate marketing services, which they provide as part of a large media package. However, there is not much evidence of success with this so far.

TradeDoubler has a more horizontal focus. Because many affiliates and marketers use other mediators, media agencies, TradeDoubler has agreements with many media agencies to use TradeDoubler's platform. Some media agencies, however, run their own affiliate marketing programmes, and view TradeDoubler as a competitor.

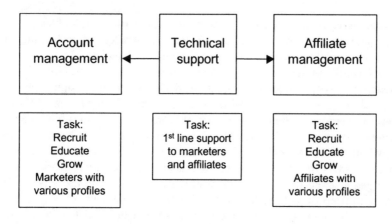

Figure 3.4   TradeDoubler's organisation in each country

TradeDoubler has structured its organisation in each country according to the needs of selling towards both marketers and affiliates, building on its mediating technology (see Figure 3.4). This allows it to serve both types of 'customers' locally. TradeDoubler's support activities are place in the head-quarters in Stockholm, where the finance department including billing procedures, and technological development, are.

Brokers' Role

Relying on its tracking technology, the broker's objective is to act as a mediator, to organise and facilitate exchanges between marketers and affiliates. An affiliate marketing broker can be compared to what Stabell and Fjeldstad (1998) call the mediator of a value network, because it relies on a mediating technology to link customers. They state that: 'the firm itself is not the network. It performs a networking service'. As a mediator, TradeDoubler's task is to admit members (marketers and affiliates) into the network that can complement each other and facilitate their interactions. Regardless of who pays for the services, TradeDoubler must recruit, educate and grow both marketers and affiliates. As put by Stabell and Fjeldstad (1998): 'Supplier–customer relationships may exist between the members of the [network], but to the mediating firm they are all customers.' According to these authors, a mediator in a value network has three primary activities:

- Network promotion and contract management
- Service provisioning
- Network infrastructure operation.

These activities provide a very accurate description of TradeDoubler's role in the network. This is reflected in the fact that TradeDoubler has built its business model to generate revenues around these activities.

Network promotion and contract management is associated with acquiring new participants to the network. Marketers must sign a physical contract to join the network, whereas it is free for affiliates to join. Affiliates have to approve an online agreement of terms and conditions, and they are quoted all commissions net, thus they never experience having to pay anything for their participation. Their earnings are simply paid into their bank account every month. According to TradeDoubler material, marketers are charged a set-up fee per country, covering initial access to the network.The value to firms of participating in an affiliate marketing network is a function of positive network demand-side externalities (Stabell and Fjeldstad, 1998; Kelly, 1998) because every time one more marketer/affiliate is added to the network it affects the value of the service to the others. With more marketers in the network, affiliates have more linking opportunities, which makes it attractive for new affiliates to join the network. Consequently, the other marketers will benefit from a larger base of affiliates, creating synergies in the network. Naturally, marketers do not want to join and allocate resources to affiliate marketing unless there are affiliates to market their products. Similarly, affiliates can't join unless there are marketer programmes to sign up with. This type of service has relatively low value to its first customers (Stabell and Fjeldstad, 1998; Kelly, 1998). TradeDoubler started up by offering its own service as an affiliate programme, where affiliates got paid for bringing in other affiliates. At the same time, TradeDoubler offered marketers to join the programme free of charge (without paying the start-up network fee). After a while, as more and more affiliates and marketers signed up it became easier to recruit more, and currently TradeDoubler Europe signs up thousands of affiliates and numerous new marketers a month.

Service provisioning consists of activities associated with establishing, maintaining, and terminating links between customers and billing for value received (Stabell and Fjeldstad, 1998). Accordingly, in TradeDoubler's network the marketers are charged a monthly fee, which covers basic servicing and training, including monthly reports and access to statistics. TradeDoubler also charges a premium on the commissions paid to affiliates.

TradeDoubler needs to ensure that interactions between marketers and affiliates run smoothly. Since affiliate marketing is run on the Internet, which is an open platform, TradeDoubler facilitates, but does not make the actual transfer of visitors between affiliates and marketers work. Likewise, TradeDoubler only facilitates, but does not enable the actual transfer of creatives (banners and images) and text. To enable this, TradeDoubler relies on the standards of the Internet. What the technology platform does is track, collect and structure these interactions. It gathers information every time an affiliate sends a visitor to a marketer through an image or link, and also registers what the visitor does once he is on the marketer's website. This information is critical to affiliate marketing, because it serves as documentation for payments from marketer to affiliate and to TradeDoubler itself. Because affiliates are paid percentages of revenues, registrations need to be made all the way from the affiliate's website up to the actual purchasing on the marketer's site, even if the visitor has spent fifteen minutes looking around the website for more information on a product.

TradeDoubler uses this information to determine how much money should be paid each month, thus billing marketer and paying out to affiliates. This information is broken down into various categories, to give marketers and affiliates a broader picture of their performance. The broker could typically give more detailed information if it wanted, which means that it has more information than any other party in the network, and thus maintains the expert role.

The above activities are standardised, but in order to be flexible, TradeDoubler offers and charges for consulting, for training and other services beyond the basic, as well as advising parties on which types of partners to form relationships with. The broker role means that it 'knows' which firms are in the network and what their characteristics are. It advises marketers personally (based on a monthly consulting fee) on which types of programmes they should offer to get the affiliates they want. It can tell them which trends are occurring in the network, and how certain types of affiliates possess different types of audiences. Given previous experiences, TradeDoubler helps marketers define objectives for their programmes and set the payment structure accordingly. These objectives are quite dependent on the marketer's products and services. Most marketers view it as one of TradeDoubler's functions to have the knowledge to help them in this regard and expect them to be of service. This is also one of TradeDoubler's additional services.

Network infrastructure operations consist of activities associated with maintaining and running physical and information infrastructure (Stabell and Fjeldstad, 1998). The TradeDoubler technology platform is updated on an ongoing basis, adding new features as the software develops. Due to the complexity of handling hundreds of thousands of relationships, the software is standardised and relatively simple for each individual relationship. There is still a potential for much development in providing more flexibility in the relationships, which is slowly being built in over time. Similarly, the amount of information that could principally be gathered and utilised from all these relationships is daunting, and TradeDoubler only analyses a selected portion of it. The firm is constantly working to build better information management features into the software, aligned with emerging needs of affiliates and marketers.

3.5   INTERACTIONS

In this section we cover the interactions that take place among participants in the network. Of interest is the actual process in which relationships are formed and ended between firms, since this forms the basis for future interactions. Additionally, we examine the series of interactions that take place on an ongoing basis. In these *activity chains*, according to Håkansson and Snehota (1995): 'several companies are linked into a sequence where activities of a company build on those performed by others and enter into those of yet others'. Activities can be defined as a sequence of acts, directed towards a purpose (ibid.). These interactions are the basis upon which the network exists.

Forming and Ending Relations

Relationships between marketers and affiliates are formed in the following sequence:

1. A marketer arranges with TradeDoubler to offer a specific programme, including:
    a. Products/services offered and/or other goals, e.g. memberships
    b. Commission structure for affiliates
    c. Banners, icons and text that affiliates can use on their own websites
2. The programme is published on TradeDoubler's and the marketer's websites
3. Affiliates sign up for the programme
4. Marketers accept or reject the application.

What happens here is that marketers, in collaboration with the broker, determine the objectives for their affiliate marketing participation and structure their programme based on this. Some marketers include all their products in their programme on the same commission structure (e.g. 7 per cent of all sales), while others only choose to include specific products and services, or differentiate the commissions in accordance with each of the products. It should be noted, though, that many merchants vary the overall commission rate (for clicks, leads and sales) among affiliates depending on their previous performance. Affiliates looking to sign up for a programme can go to the TradeDoubler's website and see all active programmes. They can visit the marketers' websites and determine which one/ones they think will produce the best results for them. There are no limits to how many programmes an affiliate can sign up for. Thus, affiliates sometimes have relationships with several marketers to sell their products/services. On average, an affiliate has relationships with 3–4 marketers. Marketers have many more relationships, due to the sheer number of affiliates in the network.

When the affiliate applies and the marker accepts, a relationship is initiated. As the relationship develops, activity links and resource ties are formed between the two companies (Håkansson and Snehota, 1995). These links and ties make up what is referred to as a 'quasi-organisation'. While the links and ties are necessary in order to facilitate the value participants desire, they also require effort to develop and maintain. Particularly with the number of relationships some marketers have, it is necessary that transaction costs are minimised. Hence, one of the broker's critical functions is to keep administration of relationships to a minimum for marketers, via its software platform. Thus, the process of forming relations among network parties is standardised and requires few resources. This also means that the terms of the relation are standardised, as it is deemed as much too demanding for marketers to negotiate terms with the majority of its affiliates, many of which will never generate much revenue. TradeDoubler does allow marketers to differentiate among their affiliates, and the technical platform supports segmenting affiliates according to their performance. The segmentation typically rewards affiliates that have high 'conversion rates' from clicks and leads to sales, in order for marketers to try and keep them loyal.

The process of forming relationships in affiliate marketing varies from traditional marketing practices in that there is a minimum of centralised decision making on the part of the marketer as to which 'properties' to market on. Typically in offline marketing and online banner advertising, marketers (or their advertising/media agencies) select the specific 'properties' they want to advertise in, usually based on demographics, psychographics and even behavioural data on the 'property's' users, which is matched with the marketer's own objectives (Corey, 1992). These data are often elaborate, leading marketers (or their consultants) to pick and choose individual publications (e.g. magazines, newspapers, TV channels), on which to place their advertisements. Publications gather data and set prices, but let marketers do the choosing.

In contrast, marketers in an affiliate marketing programme offer their programmes, and then let affiliates apply to the programme. This is central to the very nature of an affiliate marketing network. The formation of relations occurs 'bottom-up', in which the smaller affiliates choose the large marketers. While there are affiliates as large as some marketers, as stated earlier there are approximately 1,000 times as many affiliates as marketers. Instead of 500 marketers choosing which of 400,000 media firms/websites to advertise on, the 400,000 websites each choose which marketer to advertise for. However, before a relationship is created between marketer affiliate, the marketer must manually accept the affiliate's application, so there is a mutual acceptance of the relationship. This is important, as Håkansson and Snehota (1995) put it: 'a relationship between two companies cannot be unilateral, it requires co-alignment of the two parties'. In any case, it should be acknowledged that large media firms in the realm of advertising actively target marketers through salespeople and provide them with user characteristics, but this is often based on a broad effort. Since the performance-based structure makes it likely that an affiliate gets accepted to work with the marketers it wants to, it chooses the one or few marketers that it thinks will create the best match. Marketers do actively recruit specific media to their affiliate programmes, but only when they are easily identified, and when the marketer considers that specific website critical to have a partnership with. These types of websites are almost always 'Super Affiliates'.

The affiliate marketing programme/network would not look like it does if the formation of relationships was based on a top-down procedure. If websites/media firms set their rates and marketers chose which ones to market through (as banner ad networks do), each marketer would choose much fewer and predominantly larger affiliates. This is because marketers simply do not have resources to find, for example, 2,000 focused media/affiliates and replace them on an ongoing basis.

It is easy for marketers and affiliates to end relationships with each other. Marketers just have to click a button 'relationship ended' in their affiliate programme, and all affiliates have to do is remove pictures and hyperlinks to a marketer's website, and the relationship ends. There is no obligation to give notice to the marketer or broker ahead of time. These rules are specific to TradeDoubler's network, but brokers in the USA have very similar procedures (Helmstetter and Metivier, 2000). In principle, affiliates could be required to post marketers' ads for a specified amount of time, much like in traditional advertisement booking, but this would defeat the purpose of one of the keystones of affiliate marketing – performance-based payment. If affiliates were forced/obliged to carry marketers' ads for a certain period of time, they would require payment just for having the ads, since they could not remove them if they were ineffective. Similarly, if the marketer paid a high click commission, and the clicks never resulted in any sales, the marketer would prefer to end the relationship or least change commission structure. Evidently, a necessary criterion for affiliates accepting performance-based payment with no money up-front is that they have the flexibility to remove ads that do not work. Naturally, their 'ad space' is a valuable commodity to them, and they want to make sure it does not go to waste. The attention span of their users is likewise important, which is why they do not want too many integrated links either.

While affiliates can exit the network instantly, the marketer and TradeDoubler sign a contract that the marketer must give three months notice to end the relationship with TradeDoubler. Within these three months the marketer pays the monthly service fee even if the programme is not active. In practice, the marketers' links and affiliate relationships could be terminated instantly, but TradeDoubler has included an exit cost to tie marketers to the network and compensate for the turbulence and bad will that occurs when thousands of links on affiliates' websites suddenly become invalid.

While it may be a potential irritant for marketers that affiliates can remove their offers without notice and vice versa, for the network as whole we see it as a big benefit. The process can be viewed as an evolutionary process, where only the best ads, offers and products remain active in the network, while the others are not used. Naturally, affiliates are interested in making money, and they only do this if they get results. Affiliates – many of which are small – get enough information from TradeDoubler and their own records to get a good idea of which ads/offers get results, and which do not. Over time, affiliates select out the links that do not generate traffic and use only the ones that do.

Ongoing Processes

The firms in an affiliate marketing network participate in interactions, causing a flow of information and resources. The ongoing relations between parties in the network can be split into three key processes:

- Transaction The interaction between the end-user, affiliate and marketer
- Payment The transferral of money between the parties
- Information The processing and transferral of information among parties.

While the exact characteristics of these processes depend on the nature of the specific firms involved, TradeDoubler's platform standardises them to a large degree. Since all three processes are carried out through this platform, we are able to generalise them somewhat for all firms in the network. Figure 3.5

illustrates the transaction process involving end-user, affiliate, marketer and the broker.

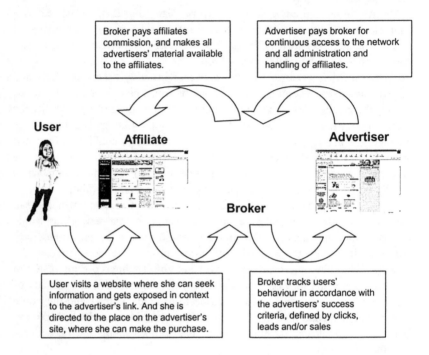

Figure 3.5   The transaction process in an affiliate marketing network

The transaction process starts at the affiliate, where its users visit the site. These users are presented with some type of message promoting the marketer, usually concentrating on specific products or services, e.g. a book title. This message can be in the form of a picture, logo or text – often a combination. Users that are interested in the message can choose to click on the hyperlink and are taken to a web page, usually where they can sign up for a product or service, purchase a product or service, or register as a member with the marketer. In generally, this web page is on the marketer's website, and clearly marked as such. However, in principle the user could be sent to another web page on the affiliate's website, as long as the user is asked to perform a transaction that has value to the marketer. Once the user has performed this transaction (or chosen not to), the process is complete. The user either moves back to the affiliate's site, continues at the marketer's site, or goes elsewhere. The broker tracks this process from the time the user clicks on the hyperlink at the affiliate's site, until the user leaves the marketer's site. A possible registration or purchase can thus be identified and measured by the broker. This tracking is done automatically and processed by TradeDoubler's software.

The payment process is purely performance-based, and thus differs from many other marketing/advertising arrangements. It starts with the end-user performing a transaction, defined by click, lead or sale. At the end of each month, the marketer pays the broker for the performance in that month, including affiliates and the broker's commissions. The broker then pays the affiliates their commission in their bank accounts monthly or on a bimonthly basis. It is the marketer's responsibility to get money from the consumer/end-user for purchases.

Affiliates are not paid before the broker receives payments from marketers. And for the same reason marketers have the possibility of cancelling affiliates' commissions if the lead or the sale is invalid. In such cases marketers cancel the transaction in their own system, which is built to automatically cancel the order in the affiliate marketing programme, and the commission is erased from the affiliate's account.

The information process consists of collecting data from the network, most of which goes through the broker, due to its tracking technology. Marketers and affiliates each have their own password that gives them access to their account. The marketer's data are broken into several standardised reports, stating the performance per impression, per click, per lead, and per sale for each affiliate, for each graphical element, per chosen time period, etc. The reports are structured according to the performance criteria set by the marketer. Affiliates' accounts are less specific, they have data for each marketer they link up to, and statistics of transactions delivered to each marketer.

Because of the shared risk and performance-based payment structure, there is an incentive for parties in the network to share some information. If marketers know more about affiliates' users, they can structure more appealing offers for products and services. If affiliates know more about marketers' products and services, they can better market these to their users in the right contexts (for example by writing specialised product reviews focusing on their users' needs). Since they share revenues for sold products and services, both parties have an interest in increasing sales. The consequence of this is that particularly affiliates actively seek out information on marketers' products and services to increase their own sales.

3.6   NETWORK CHARACTERISTICS

We examine the network according to its key characteristics. A number of researchers (e.g. Burt, 1992; Hall, 1996; Håkansson and Snehota, 1995; Alexander, 1995) have identified characteristics upon which a description of an inter-organisational network can be based. According to Hall (1996), the research findings on the area are highly fragmented, and there is no universal framework. We find that some of these researchers focus too strongly on social characteristics, which are marginal in an affiliate marketing network. Similarly, a large part of the studies are developed from observations in public policy networks, and thus they focus on somewhat different characteristics than those, which are interesting in relation to the analysis of a marketing/media network. Hence we believe an affiliate marketing network is somewhat different from the social networks described in most research and that it can best be described through a synthesis of several of these frameworks, rather than a single one. We have chosen six basic characteristics on which to base our description:

- Structure (Alexander, 1995). Refers to the number of links between firms in the network, as well as the degree to which firms are structured around a central 'core' of firms.
- Symmetry (Håkansson and Snehota, 1995; Hall, 1996 – referred to as 'reciprocity'). Reflects the degree to which firms are balanced in terms of resources and initiative.
- Continuity (Håkansson and Snehota, 1995). Refers to the length of time and stability in which relations/links exist.
- Interdependence (Hall, 1996; Alexander, 1995). Covers the degree to which firms depend on each other for resources, and the criticality of the relationships/transactions to firms.
- Standardisation (Alexander, 1995; Håkansson and Snehota 1995 – referred to as 'routinisation'). Refers to the degree to which the transaction processes and resources transacted are standardised in fixed procedures.
- Adaptation (Håkansson and Snehota, 1995). Reflects how firms in the network adapt to each other. It also reflects on how the network as a whole adapts to a changing environment (Hall, 1996).

Structure

A key observation of an affiliate marketing network is that the vast majority of firms do not have relations with each other. For example, affiliates do not interact with each other, and only a few marketers do, initiated by the broker.

However, the broker interacts with them all. This gives the broker a central position in the network, being the party that facilitates communication and transaction among the other parties. This is not unusual, though, since networks are often integrated by a centrally located organisation (Hall, 1996; Stabell and Fjeldstad, 1998). Particularly in the specific type of network structure that affiliate marketing is – an implementation set – it is natural for the implementation of the programme in question to be facilitated by an accountable party (Alexander, 1995). Centrality in a network typically translates into power, with the parties most central in relation to the flow of information and resources having the most power (Hall, 1996).

The consequence of this power is that the broker has a central position in shaping the network. Because of its technical platform and communications processes with the other parties, it makes the network function. The broker controls much of what goes on in the network from its perspective, and thus dictates what information is shared and which new parties are accepted. Belonging to the affiliate marketing platform makes it easy to add or replace partners within the network, which many firms do. Also, while all three main firm types transact with each other, it is important to note that affiliates do not communicate directly with marketers, all communication goes through the broker and is for the most part standardised. So while it is valuable to the network that choice and use of ads, images and offers are decentralised (to affiliates), this is still within the boundaries that the broker allows, for good and bad. Despite this, the broker is dependent on the results generated via the network, and thus has no apparent reason to prevent affiliates and marketers from forming and maintaining successful relationships.

Symmetry

An important characteristic of an affiliate marketing network is that affiliates usually have relationships with a select few marketers (3–4 on average), while marketers typically have relationships with hundreds or thousands of affiliates. This says something about the symmetry of relationships between affiliates and marketers. In the vast majority of cases, the marketer is larger and has more resources than its affiliates. This is somewhat different from much traditional offline advertising or banner advertising, where media companies are often as large as marketers. According to research firm Jupiter Communications (2000a), 71 per cent of online advertising goes to the top fifteen websites, while the fifteen highest spending marketers stand for only 21 per cent of online advertising spending. This indicates that for banner advertising, media firms are more concentrated than marketers. Affiliate marketing is different, though. While many large media companies do belong to TradeDoubler's programme, the majority are smaller websites that would not normally be able to generate advertising revenues. According to Håkansson and Snehota (1995), this is not the norm for business relations, which are often balanced in terms of resources and initiative taking. In this sense, the relationship between marketers and the small affiliates resembles a B2C (business-to-consumer) relationship, where the one party is much stronger than the other. This is in line with the characteristics of many of the smaller websites/affiliates, which are run by private people not otherwise considered 'firms'. The imbalance of resources among inter-organisational parties sometimes leads to an imbalance of power, which enables an organisation to use its resources to control the relationship (Hall, 1996; Alexander, 1995). However, it is not the amount of resources per se that gives a party power, but rather the dependence of one party on the other (Hall, 1996). This implies that marketers do not (only) control relationships because they are larger, but also because they have many more relationships than affiliates, and are thus much less dependent on a single relationship.

Continuity

Another aspect of the network is the level of continuity in the relationships. According to the research of Håkansson and Snehota (1995), continuity of a relationship is a key determinant of the amount of value it creates: 'there are some indications that the age of a relationship is a prerequisite for a more extensive use by the parties involved and its continuity being a precondition for change and development'. Although the TradeDoubler network has only existed in Europe since 1999, we see that many of its early relations among marketers and affiliates remain in action. While traditional advertising booking is often based on short-term agreements (ad campaigns), affiliate marketing relationships are ongoing and intended to be long-term. Ad campaigns focus at least somewhat on awareness building and branding effects and thus have different marketing objectives than affiliate marketing partnerships, but both can be useful. In any case, the characteristics of a marketing network based on long-term relationships have an influence on how the involved parties transact their business.

Particularly interesting is the fact that marketers and affiliates do not have to maintain long-term relationships. Either party can end the relationship at any time. The fact that they do remain in action for relatively long periods of time indicates that both parties feel they have something to gain from long-term relationships. The fact that they can end relationships, in principle, at any time, does not mean that it does not have costs for them to do so. Firms in relationships build up path dependencies (Håkansson and Snehota, 1995), making it difficult for them to switch partners. The more they 'learn' to act in a certain way in relation to their partner, the more they have invested in the partnership. We found that some affiliates spent a lot of time testing different products and messages from their marketer in relation to the needs of their own audiences. Switching to a new marketer would mean starting again.

It becomes apparent that all parties involved are interested in building long-term, continuous relationships, since the performance/success of an affiliate–marketer relationship often increases over time. This is due to several factors. First of all, affiliates have to experiment with different images and products from a marketer, in order to find the ones that their visitors react best to. Second, they have to find the right placement of these images and links, preferably integrated in their own content. Finally, as regular visitors see the marketer's name over time in connection with the affiliate's brand, it increases the credibility of the marketer. Visitors start seeing it as the affiliate's partner. Generally, the first three months after a new marketer join an affiliate network do not generate much revenue. Thereafter, the revenues typically increase on a continuous basis. Hence, in the beginning, the marketer's goal is to recruit a large affiliate base. When the marketer has reached a critical mass of affiliates, they can start exploiting the potential. Figure 3.6 illustrates the typical development process for affiliate marketing relationships, where firms first determine benefits, then start investing time in learning about each other. Only then do firms adapt to each other and intensify learning. Finally, a period of stability is reached, where the relationship performs well. If either of the parties is unhappy or requirements change, then the relationship can end at any time.

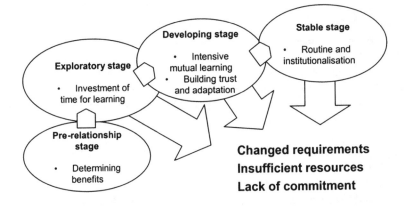

Source: Adapted from Ford et al., 1998

Figure 3.6   The development of affiliate marketing relationships

The drawback of long-term relationships is that the selection process is not as effective as it perhaps could be. While affiliates seem to be good at selecting the best offers, products and ads from a single marketer, they may not be as good at selecting the best marketer for their audience. No doubt they put some thought into choosing the best marketer for their audience when they join the programme, but surely there are factors that they didn't fully consider. Perhaps they could find an even better match by testing several marketers over a period of time to find which one the audience responds best to. Obviously there are positives and negatives of both short-term and long-term relationships. The affiliate marketing concept could, in principle, be built on short-term campaign relationships, but this may be at odds with the characteristics of performance-based payment and partnership type image marketing. In any case, both marketers and affiliates seem to be strongly in favour of keeping their relationships long-term (if successful).

Interdependence

The type of interaction between firms is a key determinant of their interdependence, and can show *why* firms set up in a certain inter-organisational structure (Alexander, 1995; Hall, 1996). The relationships between marketers and affiliates in an affiliate marketing network are more complex than they would be in a traditional advertiser–media relationship, where there is a fairly linear transaction process. Affiliate marketing on the other hand can be viewed as reciprocally interdependent. This implies that output from one firm is input for the other, and vice versa (Alexander, 1995). Correspondingly, Stabell and Fjeldstad (1998) explain the reciprocal interdependence as simultaneous activities that need to be synchronised. Specifically, affiliates may build their content around the offerings of the marketer, and marketers may determine their offerings on the basis of affiliates' content and profile. While this is true in principle, it must be noted that the inputs affiliates and marketers provide each other are not the only inputs that they use in their production. Affiliates may build some content around marketers' products, e.g. book recommendations etc., but the majority, if not all, of their content is based on other sources, e.g. news, stories, and articles. So the message that an affiliate passes on from a marketer is just one of many inputs that go into the content 'package' that meets a visitor to its website.

The difference from traditional advertising is that affiliates can, and often do, build some of their content around individual marketers' messages. While media firms in traditional advertising set-ups certainly do build their content around ads, they usually do not build it around individual ads. For example, newspapers allow for ads in various places through the pages, but do not usually write their articles based on specific ads on a certain day. Affiliates, on the other hand, can write hyperlinks to a marketer's website into their articles, or they can insert images around a relevant article. In principle, newspapers or magazines could write ads into their articles as well, but there are several reasons why this typically does not happen. One of the main reasons is because of the different payment structure of affiliate marketing versus traditional media booking. Print media are typically paid according to rates set for the amount of space given to advertisers (columns, rows, etc.), while affiliates are paid on commission for generated transactions. For a newspaper or magazine it would probably be too time-consuming to negotiate the advertising value of a single word or two in an article, which would be set at a fixed price, but for affiliates it does not really matter. All they need to know is that they get a commission on every sale, and then they can decide themselves whether it is worthwhile for them to put links to marketers into their articles. Note that this does invoke a serious ethical consideration for marketers and affiliates, which we will get into in Chapter 5 when analysing affiliates' strategic considerations.

Another important consequence of reciprocal interdependence is that affiliate and marketer can benefit from working together. According to Alexander (1995), coordinating transactions becomes more difficult under these circumstances because there is not just one single transfer of input, but rather several transfers back and forth. If the concept is utilised fully, marketers and affiliates should both adapt their respective offerings and content to each other. This does not happen fully today, in part because of the restrictiveness of TradeDoubler's communications platform. There just aren't ample means for affiliates to contact marketers and ask them to provide special offers and services that match their content and audience's needs. Affiliates do not have direct contact with marketers, as they only communicate with TradeDoubler, which only has standardised procedures for bringing affiliate requests on to marketers, but not sufficiently developed feedback systems to manage these kinds of direct interactive communications from affiliates to marketers on a large scale. For now, while affiliates would like a tighter cooperation with marketers to make better offerings and match it with content, marketers do not have the resources for this, and do not find it cost-effective anyway. They have too many affiliates, many of which are too small to deal with individually. Perhaps if/when affiliate marketing revenues for marketers increase substantially in the future, they will be willing to allocate more resources for tighter interaction with affiliates. Also, for this to be achievable, TradeDoubler must make this feedback system possible in its platform, which is not without a risk of being bypassed, and in such a case, TradeDoubler might lose control over the relationships.

Standardisation

The fact that all processes (including the set-up process) are standardised by TradeDoubler is important. It is done to maximise efficiency, i.e. to minimise transaction costs between marketers and affiliates (and the broker). According to Stabell and Fjeldstad (1998): 'Standardisation enables the mediator to match compatible customers and to effectively maintain and monitor the interaction between them'. If marketers and affiliates had to negotiate each deal and communicate personally, it would draw massive resources from marketers, who each have hundreds or thousands of affiliates. Inter-organisational contracts are both expensive to make and to enforce (Williamson, 1981). Especially for the smaller affiliates, it would not pay for marketers to allocate resources to deal with each of them on an ongoing basis. Hence, there are strong economies of scale and scope in participating in a network of affiliate marketing relationships. Once the marketer allocates the necessary resources to develop suitable offers, create hyperlinked images and generally learn the workings of the system, it can add more affiliates with relatively much fewer added resources.

Because of the standardisation of processes, there is relatively little social interaction in the network. Most affiliates have never personally met anyone at TradeDoubler or the marketers they work with. Affiliate marketing is an area that differs greatly from other types of business relationships in this regard. Typically, business relationships have a strong social element in them (Håkansson and Snehota, 1995; Burt, 1992). According to Håkansson and Snehota (1995): 'The individuals involved in a business relationship tend to weave a web of personal relationship, and this appears to be a condition for the development of inter-organisational ties between any two companies'. Not only does the standardisation of processes make social encounters unnecessary, but also the high number of relationships TradeDoubler and marketers have make them impractical. Marketers do meet with TradeDoubler and some of the 'Super Affiliates' to make special agreements, but not with the many small affiliates. According to Forrester Research (1999), most small affiliates generate very little traffic and cannot individually justify much attention from marketers. Hence, standardised business agreements are becoming increasingly possible to perform effectively with the development of the Internet and related technology, such as TradeDoubler's software platform. While they may not be as flexible as those relationships with strong social ties, they are much cheaper to maintain.

Adaptation

An important feature of a network is its ability to adapt to changing circumstances, both among firms within the network as well as for the network as a whole to its surrounding environment (Alexander, 1995; Hall, 1996). As already described, the broker mediates the network interactions, mainly based on its technical platform. Within the constraints of this platform affiliates, marketers, and the broker seek to maintain and develop relationships. Hence, learning possibilities in the network are important, in order to adapt to the development/changes of needs among network participants. This type of adaptation/learning can take place in two ways: single-loop and double-loop (Argyris and Schön, 1978; Choo, 1998).

In single-loop learning, firms correct for anomalies in performance and adjust actions without causing any change to their theory of action (Choo, 1998). Double-loop learning is adaptive to anomalies and restructures norms and associated strategies. In relation to an affiliate marketing network, we regard single-loop learning as the trial and error process that takes place in individual marketer–affiliate relationships in order to optimise performance. Double-loop learning we regard as the broker's ability to adapt the assumptions of the network and its technical platform to new demands in the network and potentially new network participants. Figure 3.7 illustrates how the two modes of learning fit together.

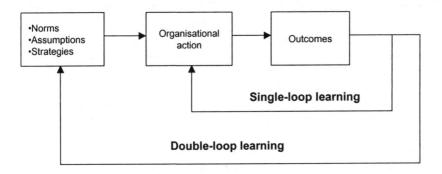

Source: Adapted from Choo, 1998

Figure 3.7   Single- and double-loop learning in an affiliate marketing network

Single-loop learning is based on affiliates' and marketers' trial and error process, where higher performance functions as the incentive to continuous adaptation. Since the outcome of the actions is standardised via the broker's technical platform, the results are easily communicated between the participants in the network, and the process of creating new explicit knowledge comes from bringing together existing explicit knowledge from a number of sources (Choo, 1998). Nonaka and Takeuchi (1995) refer to this conversion process as 'combination', where individuals exchange and combine their explicit knowledge. This allows the system to pinpoint which affiliates and which links are generating sales, and the marketer can use the data to develop new ways to increase sales. Similarly, affiliates can automatically pinpoint which links to marketers perform the best and they can use that data to improve their performance.

Even though affiliates and marketer in TradeDoubler's network have access to real time data that compromise data for better decision making in the short run, via its standardised technical platform, there is still a risk that the platform is not sufficient to base long-run decision making on. According to Choo (1998): 'Critics of standardised procedures blame them as the cause of organisational stasis inertia. Overly rigid routines can block organisational learning, stifle creativity, and forfeit organisational flexibility'. In this case the 'organisation' is the network.

Because of the risk that the assumptions behind the organisational actions do not continue to match the needs of the marketers and affiliates, TradeDoubler must 'continually construct, test, and restructure its theory of action if it is to learn and adapt (and thus survive) in a changing environment' (Choo, 1998). This is the foundation of double-loop learning, continuously redefining the organisation's theory of action.

This kind of learning is concerned with converting tacit knowledge into explicit knowledge. Nonaka and Takeuchi (1995) call this conversion process 'externalisation', which is triggered by dialogue or collective reflection. Therefore, the broker's challenge is to collect inputs both from marketers and affiliates and use them in its development of the network and the technical platform. TradeDoubler upgrades its technical platform on an ongoing basis, and the changes/improvements are based on inputs from local offices and from the system developers placed in TradeDoubler's headquarters in Stockholm. In principle, the local offices are structured to generate feedback both through affiliate management and account (marketer) management. According to an affiliate manager of TradeDoubler:

> We have dialogues with both affiliates and marketers every day, and every time we discover or receive a good suggestion from an affiliate on new features to the platform, we can email the information to our 2nd line technical support department in Stockholm, who together with the development team make the final decision whether to integrate it in the platform, and make it available for everybody in the network.

Even though TradeDoubler has made it possible to give feedback internally, the actual process depends on each affiliate/account manager's incentive to pass the information on to the development department. In the single-loop learning process, there is a natural incentive for the affiliate and the marketer to use data and improve performance due to the reward system. However, it is not an easy task to create explicit incentives for employees to actively participate in the upgrading of the platform. Hence, double-loop learning is far less frequent and developed.

3.7   CHAPTER CONCLUSION

Affiliate marketing typically takes place in the context of a large network with many thousands of firms. There are three types of participant firms in this network: marketers, affiliates and a broker. A marketer can in principle be any firm that wants to reach an interest group online, but is typically a firm wanting to sell products or services to consumers. A marketer's role in the network is to provide affiliates with marketing messages that consumers find interesting, thus enticing them to act on the message. Additionally, marketers need to formulate performance criteria for clicks, leads and/or sales that provide affiliates with incentives to invest time in developing the relationship.

Numberwise, affiliates make up the vast majority of all firms, and they are typically much smaller than marketers. An affiliate can in principle be any size or type of website, as long as it is not deemed 'unethical' by the broker or marketer. Websites are typically segmented into three types of affiliates – hobby sites, vertical sites and 'Super Affiliates'. An affiliate's role in the network is to provide a steady flow of potential end-users for the marketer. It does not necessarily need heavy traffic – a smaller, but narrower, audience can be much more effective. Affiliates draw an audience because they provide content that users seek out. It is important that they know their audience so they can select marketing messages that are relevant, thus ensuring higher revenues for themselves and marketers.

A broker is the company that maintains the platform and facilitates transactions. It should recruit both marketers and affiliates on an ongoing basis, as the affiliate marketing network is dependent on a critical mass of participants of both types. Furthermore, the broker needs to make sure that transactions run smoothly, and that they are measured correctly.

The forming of relations in affiliate marketing take place 'bottom-up', in which marketers publish programmes and affiliates choose which marketers to work with. The decisions are thus somewhat decentralised, in that 400,000 affiliates evaluate options, rather than 500 marketers, who do not have the resources to personally evaluate the marketing 'match' with so many small websites. The ending of relationships can occur instantly by either marketer or affiliate, and requires no justification.

The central ongoing process in the network is the transaction, which occurs when a user is exposed to a message from the marketer and chooses to click on it, thus being transferred to the marketer's website. This is referred to as a 'click' and may qualify as a commission-generating transaction, if it is part of the partnership's predefined objective. The user is usually transferred to a place at the marketer's website where he can register information (a 'lead') or purchase a given product or service (a 'sale'). Affiliates usually get commission on leads and/or sales. Commission is paid monthly or bimonthly from the broker to affiliates, after having received payments from the marketer based on performance statements from the broker.

In an affiliate marketing network, the vast majority of firms do not have relations with each other. Hence, the broker has a central position, because it is the only firm that interacts with all other firms. The broker also has access to the most information and makes decisions about which firms have access to the network, giving it a powerful shaping role. A difference in power is also evident in individual relationships between marketer and affiliate, because marketers are typically much larger than affiliates and also much less dependent on a single relationship than affiliates are. Marketers typically have hundreds or thousands of affiliates, many of which are very small and generate little revenue. To still make these relationships worthwhile for the marketer, and to take advantage of economies of scale in the network they need to be standardised, so that they demand very few resources. For this reason, marketer–affiliate relationships are standardised by the broker via the technology platform, hence they have relatively little flexibility and almost no social interaction.

Affiliates and marketers are reciprocally interdependent, because their content serves as input for each other. This interdependence often increases over time, as they adapt their content to each other to increase the overall effectiveness of their relationship. For this reason, affiliate marketing appears to engender long-term relationships between marketer and affiliate, the reason being that these relationships become more effective over time through an ongoing learning process. This learning takes place not only among individual relationships, but also between relationships within the larger context of the network. The broker is responsible for upgrading the network on an ongoing basis, ensuring that it adapts to changing circumstances and learns by spreading information among firms.

4. Value Creation in Affiliate Marketing

In this chapter we examine the reasons why affiliate marketing is perceived as an attractive option by its participants. This is done through an analysis of the value creation that takes place in the network. We build our research and analysis around the basic assumptions of exchange theory (Pfeffer and Salancik, 1978; Hall, 1996), arguing that firms depend on each other for resources, and thus form partnerships to gain access to them as best they can. Firms also want to ensure future access to the resources they value, and thus attempt to control them in various ways, particularly if they are rare or critical to the organisation (Pfeffer and Salancik, 1978). We define resources broadly, as being: 'Anything, which could be thought of as a strength or weakness of a given firm' (Wernerfelt, 1984). Examples of resources are raw materials, finances, personnel, services and production operations or even technological innovations (Wernerfelt, 1984). We seek to define the specific resources that firms gain access to through their participation in affiliate marketing, and determine why they are of value.

Based on this broad definition, we have identified eight key resources in affiliate marketing, through the course of our exploratory interviews with participants in TradeDoubler's affiliate network. Our research revealed 12–14 resources that could potentially be regarded as valuable to some or all firms in the network, either because they were created as a result of participants' interactions or because they were shifted among participants as a result of activity links. After initial analysis and further research we restructured and narrowed these down to a total of eight resources, which we believed all had significant impact on the value creation among firms in the network. The resources are:

- Brand. Refers to a firm's image and reputation, and can have a significant impact on the number of users both affiliates and marketers attract.
- Performance-based payment. Refers to the payment structure where affiliates are only paid when their users perform a predefined action.
- Technology platform. Refers to the technology that facilitates transactions between affiliates, marketers and the broker.

- Information. Refers to the information that is gathered by participants and/or transferred among parties.
- Brokerage. Refers to the position and activities of the broker, including the matching of parties and 'neutral' third party verification of performance.
- Context-based sales. Refers to the integration of a marketer's message in the actual editorial content of affiliates' websites.
- Consumer relations. Refers to affiliates' and marketers' access to and relationship with the consumer/end-user.
- Network relations. Refers to affiliates' and marketers' access to and relationship with each other.

In the following, we explain each of these resources individually and describe how they create value for participants, mainly affiliates and marketers. In practice, there are overlaps between the resources, but for explanatory and clarifying reasons, we analyse each resource individually. We also look at which parties are involved in the transaction, and how the resources are controlled. Our findings are based mainly on the results of our questionnaire, which we draw in on an ongoing basis throughout the chapter.

4.1   BRAND

A strong brand has often been referred to as a key asset of many firms (e.g. Aaker, 1991; Zyman, 1999). Particularly online, a brand may be important, because many of a firm's other assets are not visible (Lindstrom, 2001).

We have identified two key reasons why participants' brands play a role in their participation in affiliate marketing. The first is that there is an ongoing branding value that is created as a firm's brand is promoted through another firm, even though the payment structure does not reflect this directly (Neubert, 2000). The second is that in an inter-organisational relationship that targets third parties (end-users), firms can benefit (or lose) from being associated with another firm and its brand (Lindstrom, 2001). In the next two sections, we cover the issues of branding and brand association respectively.

Branding

Branding is the process with which firms attach meaning to their products and/or company (Aaker, 1991). In affiliate marketing, the branding of the marketer's and affiliate's name and/or products is an issue that both parties focus on. Affiliates show messages from marketers to their visitors, whether or nor they choose to react to the offer. Affiliates and marketers active in affiliate marketing generally agree to the statement that 'affiliate marketing helps strengthen a marketer's brand', affiliates agreeing more strongly than marketers. However, since affiliates only get paid when the visitor performs a transaction one could argue that in the instances when visitors do not perform the transaction, the marketer gets free branding (Neubert, 2000). For example, if an affiliate has an offer for the marketer on its website, some visitors may see the ad but not choose to make a transaction, for whatever reason. Perhaps the visitor wants to shop around a bit more, but notes the offer and the marketer's name and also notes the fact that the marketer is associated with a website that the visitor respects and trusts. Whereas the affiliate would receive payment for every time it showed an ad under traditional impression-based (CPM) advertising payment structures, in affiliate marketing it only gets paid when the visitor makes a transaction. This may be the case even though showing the visitor the ad has an isolated value to the marketer. In fact, several recent surveys have shown that web users do notice online ads; they just do not click on them.

Advertising research group Millward Brown surveyed nearly 17,000 web users' reactions to twelve banner ads after viewing each ad only *once*. They found that web users were on average 5 per cent more aware of the brand and 4 per cent more likely to purchase the product over a competitor's product than the control group. These statistics stand in contrast to the 0.3–0.5 per cent average click-through rate on banners (Bruner et al., 2001).

This dilemma is the opposite of the dilemma with traditional advertising formats such as print ads or even online banner ads. Here, one can argue that media are paid for branding, in that they are paid for each view made by a potential customer through a CPM payment structure. However, in this case the media do not get rewarded specifically for creating clicks, leads or sales for the advertiser. The majority of online marketers feel that each payment structure has its pros and cons, and that which one was best depended on the specific situation. Obviously, marketers involved in affiliate marketing understand the benefits of performance-based payment (or they probably would not be involved), but practically all of them also participate in advertising with CPM payment structures. Some of them even participate in online CPM payment systems in the form of banner advertising as well as affiliate marketing. According to research firm IDC (1999), marketers should see affiliate marketing as part of a broader marketing effort, and other methods should be used to create brand awareness. We cover the considerations a marketer should go through in placing affiliate marketing in its media mix in Chapters 6 and 7.

Since both affiliates and marketers agree that affiliate marketing does serve to strengthen a marketer's brand, but that they do not actually pay for this value indicates that affiliates do not have the influence in the network to push this through. According to TradeDoubler, it would be possible for affiliates to charge a small fee for each image or message of the marketer's that is shown to consumers (a small CPM charge in addition to the commission structure), and TradeDoubler's platform could handle these billings as well. Hence, we take this as a signal that marketers at this point of time have the strength to avoid paying for this value. This observation is supported by our description of the affiliate marketing network in the previous chapter, where we argued that marketers have control in the relationships due to their size and less dependence on individual affiliates. Marketers argue that affiliates are paid indirectly by getting commission on clicks, leads and sales. However, when marketers want to be present on a large affiliate site such as, for example, Microsoft's portal MSN, they have to pay either a higher click commission or combine CPM and transaction-based payments.

An obvious consequence of the performance-based payment structure would seem to be that affiliates will not market the marketer's company or general brand, unless it is specifically in connection with the sale of a product or service. Affiliates have no interest in creating brand awareness for a marketer, which is often a key objective for advertisers in traditional impression-based advertising such as TV and magazines (Forrester Research, 2001). Therefore presumably affiliates would typically focus on emphasising the benefits of the specific products they are selling, and only mention the marketer to the extent it is necessary for visitors to know who they are buying from. However, affiliates perceptibly prefer to work with well-known marketers, where it is not necessary to sell the company itself, other than to mention their name as a 'guarantee' of quality and delivery. This leads to our second brand-related observation, brand association.

Brand Association

Being associated with a well-known company can in itself have a positive branding effect on companies. According to Forrester Research (1999), strong brands are important, because they: 'help customers decide which online content and commerce to trust'. This goes for both affiliates and marketers. Just having offers from a well-reputed marketer may give a small affiliate a stamp of approval. Thus, it gives affiliates credibility to link up to a marketer with a well-known brand. Some users may not be aware of how relatively easy it is to become an affiliate for a large company. They could think that the large company has chosen the affiliate as a marketing channel for its products because it trusts the expertise and credibility of the website. No broad/mass marketer would want its brand to be associated with unethical or distrustful partners. Similarly, it gives smaller marketers (particularly online retailers) a boost to have a large affiliate/media sell its products. In TradeDoubler's network many marketers offer relatively high click-through payments to websites they particularly want to be associated with because of their reputation.

Obviously this goes the other way as well. Since users may believe that firms have specifically selected partners based on their credibility, they must take this into consideration. If users are burned by an affiliate they trusted, they may hold it against the marketer. Even worse if a marketer burns them; they will probably hold it against the affiliate that recommended their products. Being associated with an unethical partner can harm a firm's brand and have a significantly negative value (Lindstrom, 2001). A frequent argument against affiliate marketing, often stated by media agencies, is that marketers do not have enough control over their brand, and are fearful of diminishing its premium characteristics.

This issue goes to the heart of the top-down versus bottom-up decision-making discussion. If a company wants to control all aspects of its environment, it has to maintain a top-down decision-making process (Mintzberg et al., 1998). On the other hand, companies that decide to decentralise some of the decision-making beyond their own boundaries have to give up some control. Some initiatives can be taken to limit the damage that can be done by other parties, but the risk is always there. If a marketer carefully evaluates each and every partner it wants to work with, it would never have the resources to work with so many small partners, such as the hobby websites. With the benefits of a distributed network of specialised partners come the drawbacks of living with the uncertainty of how they might act. We cover this issue as part of a marketer's considerations for adopting affiliate marketing in Chapter 6.

While media agencies and marketers may feel that affiliate marketing just needs to mature, we argue that there is a fundamental difference between affiliate marketing and impression-based advertising. This difference will not go away, no matter how much affiliate marketing grows, and the fundamental issue is not really about technology. Large-scale marketers and their media agencies are used to developing elaborate plans for their clients' marketing, based on large amounts of research (Corey, 1992). Planning works well in relatively simple environments, but less well in complex environments with a lot of uncertainty (Mintzberg et al., 1998). In an environment as complex and dynamic as an affiliate marketing network, with 400,000+ affiliates, extensive planning becomes infeasible, or at the very least, ineffective. How can any marketer monitor and control thousands of individual partners on a continuous basis? Many marketing academics and practitioners (e.g. Brown, 1995; Ogilvy, 1990) argue that marketing has run its course with regards to developing elaborate plans and research, and marketers should rather focus on neglected aspects of marketing, such as relationship-building. Trust and commitment are closely linked in business relationships (Ford et al., 1998), and affiliates will probably be unwilling to dedicate the resources necessary to build successful long-term relations if they are not given some leeway within which to act. As long as some marketers and media agencies insist on controlling all aspects of their brands (whether justifiably or not), they will probably never find a public affiliate marketing programme an attractive option.

Note that we are not saying a firm's brand is not important, just that in certain environments it may be difficult and unproductive to try and control it too tightly. Because users probably regard marketers and affiliates to be in more of a long-term partnership than traditional advertisers and media, the risk of getting hurt by the other party's mistakes is higher than for traditional advertisers, although this is not totally without risk either. Another risk is that marketers that have spent a lot of resources building a tightly controlled image and positioning for their brand could see the brand become diluted if they form partnerships and become associated with affiliates with conflicting images. In principle, marketers will never be partnered with affiliates they have not manually accepted, but in practice thorough evaluation of thousands of affiliates is a resource-demanding process.

4.2   PERFORMANCE-BASED PAYMENT

The payment structure is characterised as perhaps the most important factor in affiliate marketing (Jupiter Communications, 1998b; Helmstetter and Metivier, 2000). It differs from traditional advertising/media booking in that affiliates are not paid a predefined amount, but rather paid according to predefined performance criteria after the time period in question. This makes affiliates accountable for their performance, and they are paid accordingly. While this is a shift from much of the logic of traditional advertising, it may become standard in the future, as technology makes it feasible (Cartellieri et al., 1997; Jupiter Communications, 2000a). McKinsey consultants Cartellieri et al. (1997: 44) make the following statement:

> As the technology improves, the impact of Internet advertising will increase and become easier to measure, and the gap between this new precise, interactive marketing capability and conventional 'fuzzy' passive media will widen. Over the next few years, advertising agencies and consumer marketers will be under pressure to change their whole approach to marketing communications.

In fact, this trend is already evident, and Forrester Research (2001) argues that it will continue in the future. The research firm argues that full or partial performance-based marketing spending will increase from 62 per cent of all online marketing spending in 2000 to 82 per cent in 2003.

Risk sharing has often been held up as the main reason why the performance-based payment structure is valuable. Affiliate marketing is promoted because marketers 'only pay for what they get' (Jupiter, 1998b; IDC, 1999). Instead of marketers paying a fixed fee for advertising, they only pay their marketing expenses if they achieve a predefined objective. Hence the risk is shifted, at least partially, from marketer to media/affiliate. Another factor that has been mentioned is that the performance-based payment structure gives affiliates more motivation to help marketers achieve success, since the risk-shift means that their interests are aligned (Helmstetter and Metivier, 2000; Maloney, 2001). Finally, an area that hasn't been addressed much in the affiliate marketing literature, but which we uncovered during our general description of the network, is the value of a 'bottom-up' decision-making process where a large number of decision-making units (affiliates) have an incentive to actively improve their performance. This creates what is often referred to as 'smart' network effects (Kelly, 1998). As a consequence, our discussion of performance-based payments focuses on risk sharing and on interest alignment.

Risk Sharing

A valuable aspect for marketers of affiliate marketing is that they can match their marketing expenses to revenues and customer acquisition (Jupiter Communications, 1998b). The risk factor is reduced, because marketers shift some of the risk of failure to affiliates (Cartellieri et al., 1997). Naturally, it is very valuable to marketers that their marketing payments are variable in relation to predefined criteria. Rather than spending money on advertising that they can't be sure will pay back, marketers in an affiliate marketing programme know that they only have to pay out marketing expenses as a percentage of revenues or for a lead, where most marketers have calculated conversion rates from leads to new customers, and can thus estimate the value of a lead. Hence, marketing expenses take the form of a variable cost. This is of value to marketers, especially since marketing expenses are often difficult to match to revenues and thus justify (Zyman, 1999). While many marketers spend lots of money doing research and planning marketing, advertising is still often 'hocus-pocus' without much focus on accountability. Especially in areas that marketers know relatively little about, like the Internet, a marketing system with a 'built-in' evaluation system can speed up the learning curve.

While risk is reduced for marketers, it is increased for affiliates, though, as they do not have any security for revenues ahead of time. This makes it difficult for them to plan and make budgets. Big media sites with as many as a million unique visitors a month and many employees have expenses to pay each month. And many of them rely totally on advertising for all their revenues. Typically, they use both banner advertising and affiliate marketing. With their banner advertising, they know ahead of time how much money they will make in a given month, because when they make an agreement with a marketer for this type of advertising, they arrange everything ahead of time, including how many impressions of the marketer's banner they will show, and what the CPM price is for each banner. This means that they can match expenses with revenues and cut back if necessary. With their affiliate marketing, they can never know exactly how many revenues they will generate. They know their commission rate, but they can never be sure how much revenue they will generate. They thus run the risk of not covering their expenses for a given time period, which is especially critical now that investors have really begun to focus on profitability for online businesses (Jupiter Communications, 2000a; Bruner et al., 2001). Hence affiliates cannot use a performance-based payment structure only, unless they have solid experience of stable earnings from relationships with given marketers. While marketers and brokers do not seem to believe that it is a big disadvantage for affiliates that they do not have security for fixed revenues, affiliates don't consider it as big a disadvantage as one could expect. We suspect that the main reason is that most affiliates work with both CPM-based banner advertising and affiliate links concurrently and consider affiliate marketing as an additional income generator. This is only possible because affiliate links are integrated to the content of the website, and do not necessarily take up advertising space and capacity that can be sold for campaign and awareness purposes at CPM prices. In addition, the majority of affiliates are hobby sites, and they are thus typically not dependent on a fixed income.

With the performance-based principles of affiliate marketing the media are forced to analyse the potential of their users' behaviour and preferences in order to estimate revenues. With CPM-based payments, the estimates are based on a number of visitors and approximate demographic data of the visitors, but only to a diminutive degree on the users' behaviour once they are on the affiliate site. Affiliates' desire to avoid risk is manifested by getting payment for 'clicks', which is not always included in the payment structure, depending on the marketer's objectives. A reason why affiliates should not take the full risk could be that they do not have an influence on how marketers treat end-users once they are on their website. Affiliates only have very limited influence on the final sale, if any. It would seem natural that affiliates do not want to undertake a risk, which they do not have any influence over.

Interest Alignment

The idea behind performance-based payment is that in holding affiliates accountable for their performance, it gives motivation to affiliates to actively attempt to sell the marketers' products, not just passively pass on a message (Helmstetter and Metivier, 2000). Agency theory postulates that by aligning the success of agents (affiliates) with the success of the principal (marketer), the agent works harder and more effectively to ensure the principle's success (Levinthal, 1988; Jacobides and Croson, 2001). The overall payment structure that marketers offer as part of their programmes can be viewed as a contract between principal and agent. The purpose of these contracts, from the perspective of the marketers, is to maximise their long-term payoff (Levinthal, 1988). Hence they attempt, with a lack of full information, to create incentives for affiliates that entice them to help marketers achieve this objective (Jacobides and Croson, 2001). For this reason, marketers and the broker work on developing specific performance criteria for affiliates that are aligned as closely as possible with the marketer's objectives. For example, if affiliates were simply paid a CPM rate for each message/image they showed, they would not have much incentive to try and find the message that has the most effect on its audience and thus resulted in the best promotion of the marketer. It is important to marketers that they know that affiliates have an incentive to bring them success. Because marketers have so many different affiliates, they can't possibly monitor them all. Often the only way to ensure that an agent is working in the principal's interest, when close monitoring is not an option, is to make sure they have the incentives to do so (Levinthal, 1988; Jacobides and Croson, 2001). A win/win situation, where both parties are successful, is naturally of value to all parties. In this situation the relationship between affiliates and marketers does not have to be a zero-sum game. Rather, a good payment structure can increase joint-agency value to the benefit of all parties (Jacobides and Croson, 2001). It is commonly agreed between marketers and affiliates that: 'performance-based payment leads to a closer partnership between marketer and affiliate'. A close partnership is at least an indicator of interest alignment, since parties in a close long-term partnership over time often develop a mutual dependence on each other and are thus interested in helping each other to success (Håkansson and Snehota, 1995).

Smart Network Effects

A consequence of shifting risk to affiliates is that they have an incentive to find ways to improve performance. Hence in TradeDoubler's network there are 400,000 affiliates each with an incentive to try different approaches and monitor performance, rather than just 500 marketers. An interesting effect of the 'bottom-up' decision-making described earlier is that the network becomes more dynamic and more intelligent, because there are many more decision-making points (Kelly, 1998). According to Kelly (1998), networks become more 'intelligent' the more nodes that are added, even if the individual nodes are relatively unsophisticated. He argues that: 'dumb parts, properly connected into a swarm, produce smart results'. This means that a large number of individual nodes, each working in autonomous fashion, as a system can produce results that are superior to a centrally controlled system. 'The great benefits reaped by the New Economy in the coming decades... will be due in large part to exploring and exploiting the power of decentralised and autonomous networks' (Kelly, 1998). The reason for the intelligence of a decentralised network lies in the fact that the number of decision-making units is increased dramatically, and that each individual unit/node only has to manage a very simple decision-making process.

In this fashion, a network with 400,000 decision-making affiliates can produce more effective overall results than a network where only a few hundred marketers make all the decisions. Basically, each affiliate can try out various options and measure the result. Each individual affiliate does not have to consider the results of the overall network, just its own performance. The learning comes not only from the decentralised decision making itself, but from the fact that each of the decision makers has tools for getting feedback, i.e. measuring the results and adapting if performance is unsatisfactory, through the process of single-loop learning (Argyris and Schön, 1978; Choo, 1998). Affiliate marketing can be seen as part of a larger system, where the basic output is marketing messages to end-users. The affiliate marketing network sends out these messages to its environment (end-users), and receives feedback on their effectiveness through end-users' reactions and the resulting performance.

This learning process is a key aspect of affiliate marketing. According to Mintzberg et al. (1998), the only way to become successful in a turbulent and uncertain environment where one has little knowledge is to 'learn by doing'. Firms can set out elaborate plans, but these almost always come up short in these environments. For example, many marketers had high hopes for Internet banner ads, but have been surprised by their lack of effectiveness (Bruner et al., 2001). They developed various formats and did the research, and for a while it did seem like they worked well if only marketers targeted the banners and reached the right audience. However, even the effectiveness on these banners has dropped steadily. Now firms are asking themselves whether the problem isn't with the fundamental nature of the banner ad, rather than simply with the lack of targeting (Cross, 1999). If viewers do not react to these ads, it does not matter how targeted they are. In any case, these doubts have caused many marketers to re-evaluate their online marketing plans and focus more on performance-based advertising (Jupiter Communications, 2000a). The point is that there have been questions for years about the effectiveness of CPM-based banner ads (e.g. IDC, 1999), and the websites carrying the ads didn't have much incentive to do anything as long as they were getting paid.

The assumption here is that there was not much learning taking place in these systems, for several reasons. First of all, marketers were the ones making the decisions, and they did not have the resources or the skill to fully evaluate the situation, integrate the feedback and test a variety of options (Cross, 1999). Second of all, while marketers could measure click-through rates for their banners, they maintained that they had other objectives beyond creating click-through, for example building brand awareness (which was very difficult to measure) (Warner, 1999; Neubert, 2000). While this is no doubt true, the consequence was that they didn't have the information necessary to evaluate their marketing methods against their objectives, and thus didn't have a proper feedback process.

Affiliate marketing, on the other hand, has many more decision-making nodes, and also a more elaborate feedback process, because there is more tracking performed and more data available to participants. More decision-making nodes means that there can be more variety within a system. A system typically develops/evolves through a process of variation, selection and retention (Pascale et al., 2000). The more variation there is within the system, the more likely it is that new methods emerge that make the system better suited to its environment. If there is an effective feedback process, the system is able to recognise and select these methods, and allow them to spread to the rest of the system and be retained. In affiliate marketing, the selection process takes the form of some affiliates being more successful than others in generating revenues for marketers. TradeDoubler and the relevant marketers can see which affiliates are most productive, and look on their websites to see exactly what they have been doing. This way they can develop more of the types of messages that are most effective, and assist other affiliates in best practice methods. This type of variation–selection–retention is present in practically all systems that develop over time, but it is more effective in an affiliate marketing network than in banner advertising market structures, for the reasons mentioned above. This has value for affiliates and marketers alike, because it ensures that the entire 'pie' grows as the network draws more resources from its environment when it becomes more effective at meeting their needs (Hall, 1996).

It should be noted, though, that a totally decentralised system is not always effective, and is often very inefficient (Kelly, 1998). Total autonomy can paralyse a system. As Kelly (1998) emphasises, 'without some element of guidance from the top, bottom-up control will freeze when options are many'. For this reason, it is important that there is some (general) guidance from marketers, who have a broader perspective from their many relationships with different affiliates. They do this by establishing guidelines for affiliates to act (e.g. do not lie about offers) and enforcing these guidelines by threatening to cancel affiliates that ignore them. Similarly, the broker also provides guidance for affiliates as well as marketers, in selecting which marketers and affiliates should join the network, as well as in writing contracts to be signed by marketers and affiliates on how they should behave, and finally the broker has multiple affiliate retention systems to make use of, for example newsletters, e-mails, and support mails. All parties must be aware of the risks of too much autonomy, and the necessity of some guidance by the broker. Hence, TradeDoubler set criteria and choose which affiliates and marketers should be part of the network. Consequently, TradeDoubler actively match affiliates and marketers, based on their knowledge of the network.

4.3   TECHNOLOGY PLATFORM

A prerequisite of performance-based payment is that the performance can be measured (IDC, 1999). In affiliate marketing, the measurement of end-user transactions, commonly referred to as 'tracking', is done via a software platform that is managed by the broker. Hence the characteristics and quality of this software is an integral part of the value creation process (IDC, 1999; Helmstetter and Metivier, 2000). Although this software measures the transactions, it does not facilitate them. The actual transactions take place through hyperlinks, which are a result of the interlinked characteristics of the World Wide Web and the Internet. Hence the very nature of affiliate marketing is closely linked to that of the Internet. This 'connectivity' is a key value creator for affiliate marketing. The third value element has to do with 'scalability', which has been a major focus point of affiliate marketing literature (e.g. Helmstetter and Metivier, 2000). For example, much of Amazon's affiliate marketing success has been attributed to it having more than 400,000 affiliates (Bruner et al., 2001). The Internet makes this possible with relatively little expense, because everyone is already connected. The affiliate marketing platform just needs to be built on top.

Affiliate Marketing Platform

A tracking technology is a critical part of affiliate marketing (IDC, 1999). Without the technology platform, affiliate marketing would not be possible. TradeDoubler's platform underlies the performance tracking and billing processes, and makes them run smoothly. Both affiliates and marketers agreed that TradeDoubler's technology saves time in the communication between the two parties. The reason for this is mainly that the platform is standardised so that communications, for example, applications for partnerships and monthly billings, can take place efficiently. The ongoing communications are much more cost-effective with a lot of affiliates, since the communications processes are standardised and therefore basically the same for all affiliates. Instead of having to negotiate agreements and personally handle payments and billing, it is done automatically. TradeDoubler has been continually upgrading its platform with new features. Marketers and affiliates appreciate this, since it is important to use the newest technology because the information needs develop alongside the advancement of the affiliate relationships. These features have mainly concerned a more elaborate tracking and performance statistics, making it possible for marketers and affiliates to further evaluate and optimise their relationships.

Connectivity

The advantages of the Internet itself are first and foremost that everyone is 'connected' (Kelly, 1998). Any affiliate and marketer can form a partnership easily if they want, because they are already connected (through the Internet). A simple hyperlinked word or image can transport a user directly from the homepage of one to the other. At any time, affiliates can go to a marketer's site and download images and text, and then upload it to their own website. Also, TradeDoubler tracks the performance of affiliates by routing consumers (silently) through their own hub, which also can be done because of the Internet. All these functions would be more time-consuming and therefore less feasible in other media types. Certainly, a newspaper ad or TV commercial cannot take an interested consumer directly to the marketer's brochure or store. The consequences of this is that affiliates are able to sell products and services directly, because the sale can be measured by following the consumer's path, and the commission can be attributed to the right affiliate.

Connectivity also makes it relatively cheap to publish and distribute information (Strauss and Frost, 1999). This allows people to publish narrow, specialised content that would be prohibitively expensive to print. Many people have started small niche websites covering a broad range of issues. Currently, there are millions of websites in existence (Bruner et al., 2001). In this way the Internet sets the foundation for the expert websites and communities that are a key part of the affiliate marketing concept – that affiliates use their credibility and tight consumer relations to market products to consumers (Helmstetter and Metivier, 2000).

While affiliate marketing enjoys many of the general benefits of the Internet, it also suffers from many of its downsides. These downsides are serious, and have inhibited its growth. The characteristics of the Internet play a large part in this. First of all, there are simply so many websites and pages on the Internet, that consumers have actually become wary of 'surfing the Net', which many people did when they first became acquainted with the Internet. Today, most people use a very limited number of websites, and are wary about using those they are not familiar with. A study in March 2000 by Jupiter Communications revealed that the average Internet user visits less than 20 websites on a regular basis (Bruner et al., 2001). According to a recent survey by Jupiter Media Metrix (2001), four media properties account for more than 50 per cent of the total time Americans spend online (out of the many million websites in existence). Two years ago, in March 1999, eleven media properties accounted for this much 'market share'. This is simply a reaction to the huge amount of information on the Internet. People face information overload and react by creating order in the chaos – by keeping to what they know and avoiding too much new information (Choo, 1998). The fact that many websites, including many affiliates, are littered with hyperlinks to various other websites makes it even more difficult for users to keep in control and make sure they do what they set out to. For this reason, consumers generally seem to follow a rule that they avoid clicking on unknown/new hyperlinks. They have a few websites that they generally visit, and otherwise they use a portal/search engine to find what they want (Bruner et al., 2001). People do not click on banners mainly because they do not want to be brought off-track, and affiliate marketing messages have the same problem. On the other hand, the fact that users avoid surfing the Net, but focus their attention, might be perceived a benefit for affiliate marketing if the links are implemented in a context where the user perceives them as a good recommendation to click through. Such a click-through can be assumed to derive from a natural interest on the part of the user.

Another problem the Internet causes for affiliate marketing participants is actually the opposite scenario. If an affiliate writes a book report and refers to a certain bookstore, consumers might just look for that book elsewhere for a cheaper price, since they are going to purchase through the Internet anyway. There are literally thousands of online bookstores, and shopping agents like PriceRunner (www.pricerunner.com) make it quick and simple to find the cheapest price on a given item. TradeDoubler's technology is able to track if the user comes back to the marketers within a time period, typically 14 days, from the first visit (by placing a cookie), so if he or she chooses to purchase after shopping around, the affiliate still earns a commission. Naturally, this does not help if the user finds the book cheaper somewhere else and buys it there. It should be noted, though, that a Jupiter Media Metrix survey revealed that 89 per cent of online book buyers purchase a book at the first website visited. For online travel buyers though, this figure is only 55 per cent (Baker et al., 2001).

Scalability

The key value for the broker, marketers and affiliates lies in the economies of scale, which means that marginal costs decrease as the number of units increase (Porter, 1980), and as described earlier, value increases for each new participant added to the network (Stabell and Fjeldstad, 1998). Once the technology is developed, additional parties can be added to the network at very little cost. Although this is not a new phenomenon, some writers (e.g. Kelly, 1998; Evans and Wurster, 1997; Varian, 1998) have emphasised that with information goods, economies of scale are taken to new extremes. This is because the development costs for the first product/user are huge, and each additional product/user can be added for almost no cost. Information typically has a high fixed cost of production, but a very low cost of reproduction (Varian, 1998). Basically, this means that once a marketer has paid TradeDoubler the set-up fee, and has connected the software to its own website, it can add all the affiliates it wants for free, because the standardised software is easily extended. Each affiliate can also join any marketer's programme easily and free of charge. The consequence of this is that many marketers have thousands of affiliates, maintained and administered with relatively few resources.

The technology is thus of value to marketers, as they are able to form multiple relations with affiliates for relatively little cost, and vice versa. Much of this is due to the Internet itself rather than TradeDoubler's technology. The affiliate marketing platform piggybacks on the Internet technology and specialises for its specific purpose. But without the Internet, affiliate marketing would be practically impossible. TradeDoubler would have to maintain its own network and physically connect all firms, as well as all consumers. It is therefore natural that affiliate marketing has risen as a result of the development and growth of the Internet (Helmstetter and Metivier, 2000). It is a critical success factor for the programme that firms and end-users all use the Internet on a regular basis. Since many have started to do so, it is only natural for firms to build platforms that extend its capabilities through specialisation in a certain area – in this case marketing and selling. So one could say that TradeDoubler offers not only its own platform, but the capabilities of the Internet as well, which most firms take far from full advantage of.

4.4   INFORMATION

The success of an affiliate marketing network depends on the quality of information available to the parties (Helmstetter and Metivier, 2000). Parties generate much of their own information, and some is also passed through the network. First and foremost, from a marketing standpoint, information on end-users (target groups) is valuable in the sense that it allows marketers to target their products and services better (Corey, 1992). Since interests are – in principle – aligned between affiliate and marketer, this information may not necessarily need to be exchanged. If affiliates have information on their users, they should themselves target marketers' messages to these users in a way that benefits marketers (Helmstetter and Metivier, 2000). The second important type of information is on performance, i.e. the number and types of transactions in an affiliate–marketer relationship. As we mentioned in Chapter 3, a single-loop learning process takes place between affiliates and marketers. As they can monitor their performance, affiliates in particular adjust their actions according to the feedback they get, in order to increase their performance.

End-user Information

End-user (consumer) characteristics and usage patterns are important because marketers usually aim for certain target groups with their products, and because they want to be represented in a certain context (Corey, 1992). Affiliates usually know their consumer profiles reasonably well, particularly the larger affiliates that actively gather information and send out newsletters. To the degree they know the characteristics and usage patterns of their users, this information is valuable to marketers. In traditional offline marketing and banner advertising, media firms use this information as a selling point to marketers, providing them with user information to convince them of how they may fit in with the marketer's target group. Marketers set a strategy and target group and then choose the media that are deemed the best match (Corey, 1992). With affiliate marketing, affiliates also have some of this information, but they do not pass it on to marketers directly. Instead, they use it themselves to choose the marketer(s) that they think will provide the best match with their users, thus giving them the most income. The information has the same value, but the affiliate rather than the marketer actively uses it. In connection with this issue, demographic segmentation principles cannot be replaced 100 per cent by behavioural and point-of-sale segmentation principles as it helps all parties if marketers could segment affiliates demographically more effectively, and if the affiliates know their audiences well. This indicates that there is some reservation with the total bottom-up partnership formation where affiliates choose marketers. It does appear that both parties think it is important that marketers segment affiliates demographically and target their marketing on this basis, rather than leave it all up to affiliates. This is consistent with some of the more recent experiences in the USA, which suggest that marketers should, at least in the initial selection process, turn down applications from affiliates that have audiences that are far away from the marketer's target group, in order not to waste administration resources on affiliates that do not generate revenues (Bruner et al., 2001). This selection process requires demographic information on affiliates' audiences.

A common concern often expressed by media agencies, not active in affiliate marketing, questions the value of this approach. In their opinion, the reason why affiliate marketing needs to be based on performance-based payment is because the traffic generated through an affiliate marketing network is unfocused and ineffective. This comment is in stark contrast to the intension of affiliate marketers, stating that the huge number of niche affiliates create a much more targeted traffic than would normally be the case (see, for example, Forrester Research, 1999; Helmstetter and Metivier, 2000). The media agencies argue that many of the small websites are unprofessional and do not have the information to provide marketers (or to utilise themselves) on their users that combined with a marketer's objectives can create a good match. This lack of information, as well as many small websites' lack of business competence and inability to spend the effort necessary, leads to too many bad matches where marketers' offerings are irrelevant to the consumers of many websites. While a top-down matching of marketers and media may have its flaws, they argue, at least marketers (or their media agencies) can select professional media that can show them valid information on their users. This makes the traffic generated of much better quality. According to some media agencies, marketers are able to pay fixed impression-based rates because they know that the traffic is high quality. They think traffic generated through an affiliate marketing network has a lot of waste, where users are exposed to irrelevant messages.

This is an interesting point, which makes a lot of sense. However, the affiliates and marketers active in affiliate marketing both believe that performance-based payment does create better quality traffic, otherwise they would not be active. Also, the fact that the affiliates select the marketer indicates an activity and a dedication to creating a successful media–marketer relation. Maybe the fact that a bottom-up selection process diminishes a traditional media agency's role significantly had an influence on some media agencies' opinion, consciously or otherwise. Media agencies are typically strong proponents of planning, intensive data collection and the like, since it is one of their important functions. In any case, media agencies do have a major influence on many marketers' marketing decisions, and if they use these arguments – justified or not – to argue against affiliate marketing, it will be a very real barrier to its growth if they are believed.

Performance Information

Performance information is important in that it shows affiliates which results are created from various marketers, products and message types. Based on this information, they can adjust their links to maximise overall performance. Likewise, marketers can get an overview on which affiliates they make the most money from, and which products and message types are the most attractive to their audiences. The consequence of this is that affiliates can test out a range of options in 'real time', where they almost instantly can see the results of their performance. All affiliates and marketers have their own account on TradeDoubler's website, where they can view their performance at any time. This information is valuable, because it allows affiliates to optimise their performance. This type of bottom-up approach helps marketers as well as affiliates, since they benefit from revenue increases. Detailed and specified information appear to strengthen the relationships, for example, performance statistics for each individual link, in order to get detailed information on which links create the best results.

The broker controls and initiates the information that passes through the network. Every month TradeDoubler sends out newsletters to all marketers and to all affiliates that focus on sharing some basic information with the network. Both newsletters emphasise best practice. What happens is that TradeDoubler's staff analyses performance statistics in the network (each country does this separately) to find the best performers among marketers and affiliates in relation to a number of criteria. For example, they look for which affiliates make the most money for a given marketer, or which affiliates have experienced the largest growth rate in commissions. After having identified these performers, they visit their websites and look at how they have achieved their performance. For example, if an affiliate has achieved good results by using a specific link, or marketing a product in a specific context, the newsletter describes how they have done it. While one could imagine affiliates being annoyed by their ideas being spread, they actually benefit because it gives them free publicity, and successful ideas are thus spread quickly through the network.

4.5 BROKERAGE

Since we have specifically chosen to focus on brokered affiliate marketing programmes, brokerage becomes an important aspect, since it is one of the main reasons for the existence of brokered programmes. The reason is that the broker is assumed to act as a neutral third party that both marketers and affiliates can trust (Helmstetter and Metivier, 2000). Because fees depend on actual performance, it is important to both parties that this performance is accurately measured.

TradeDoubler serves as a neutral party that measures performance and monitors the network. There is consensus among affiliates and marketers that it is important that a neutral third party verifies the results between marketers and affiliates. This is particularly important to affiliates, who often do not have the resources themselves to measure their own performance, and also cannot themselves measure what is purchased on the marketer's website. TradeDoubler provides value in the sense that many marketer–affiliate relations would never be created if it wasn't for the third-party measurement, because affiliates may not have thought they could trust marketers to accurately measure their performance. Likewise, it is critical for both affiliates and marketers; a neutral party handles the payments. Again, many smaller affiliates would probably otherwise fear that they would not get their money, and if they didn't they would not be able to do anything about it, and the marketers would easily need to employ extra resources, just to handle monthly payments to hundreds or thousands of affiliates. This is the main reason why most affiliate marketing is now done through brokers like TradeDoubler, whereas it started off as a one-to-many programme offered by large marketers to their affiliates (Bruner et al., 2001). With a broker such as TradeDoubler, marketers sign a contract agreeing to fulfil their commitments and all the standard premises. Affiliates are automatically protected by this agreement when they join the network, and TradeDoubler will enforce it if necessary, which has happened on some occasions. Affiliates do complain from time to time, and TradeDoubler takes care of it. This actually provides value for both parties in the long run, because accountability is enforced in the partnerships, and without suspicion, the trust necessary for a long-term commitment is more likely to be built (Ford et al., 1998). TradeDoubler has the legal responsibility with regard to billing and payments, so that affiliates and marketers only have a single payment and billing process, which otherwise would become very complex with thousands of relations with reciprocal processes, for example in the case of returned sales, where marketers have to cancel an affiliate's commission.

4.6   CONTEXT-BASED SALES

As mentioned in the concept description, a key characteristic of affiliate marketing is that many niche affiliates leverage their relationships with end-users to market products for marketers (Helmstetter and Metivier, 2000). When these products are closely linked to the affiliates' own content, it is often referred to as context-based selling, which is meant to lead to better results for marketers because end-users are reached in the right context (Forrester Research, 1999). However, our interviews revealed that this integration of content and commercialism also invokes strong opinions among media firms, who feel this integration may harm their credibility. There are many issues to discuss in this matter, however we cover only the issue of content integration and the issue of ethics.

Content Integration

With the notion of context-based selling, consumers are marketed products and services within the context they are already in (Forrester Research, 1999). Optimally, this means that they only receive the right marketing messages at the right time. For example, when a consumer is looking up information on French cooking, he is offered a French cookbook from an online bookstore as a supplement to the information the affiliate has. Advertising is generally more effective this way, because there is a higher probability that the message is relevant to the consumer. A survey performed by Forrester Research (1999) revealed that click-through rates for context-based links were 4 per cent for the marketers they surveyed; six times that of banner click-through rates. It is also a commonly shared notion by affiliates and marketers that performance is significantly improved when a link is integrated in an affiliate's content, and that specific product links are significantly more effective than general banner links. There is definitely consensus in the network that context-based selling offers value via higher effectiveness.

Building sales messages specifically around, and even into, media content has been promoted as one of the cornerstones of affiliate marketing (see, for example, Helmstetter and Metivier, 2000; Forrester Research, 1999). Consumers are presented with marketing messages when they are most receptive. For example, a niche site dedicated to wildlife can have an article describing how one can rent summerhouses in the area and also have hyperlinks to a company specifically renting out summerhouses. Rather than charging for advertising space, the site could simply charge commission. Consumers do not necessarily see this as a nuisance; since part of the reason why people join online communities may be that they see it as a place where they know they can find the products they seek (Hagel and Armstrong, 1997). According to Hagel and Armstrong's (1997: 148) research into online communities:

> Marketers who are quick to catch on to the potential of online advertising – advertising that is designed to stimulate sales directly and that is placed in the right context within the right community – stand to improve the effectiveness of their marketing programmes overall.

While context-based selling/marketing has been described as an important part of affiliate marketing, the degree to which affiliates embrace the full concept varies. Affiliate marketing does not demand that the concept is used in full. Some affiliates just add marketers' links to their sites as an afterthought, similar to the way they would place banner ads. Others integrate marketing messages and hyperlinks into their content. This depends largely on the type of products or services the marketers sell. The more specialised the product is, the easier it is to integrate, since product and content have to match for it to be effective (Forrester Research, 1999). Books have so far proven to be very successful at exploiting the opportunities of a broad affiliate marketing network, since they can be matched to almost any niche or hobby. Affiliates linked to a bookstore can find books that are closely linked to their niche, and thus presumably of interest to their audience, almost no matter how specialised they are. Other marketers have just a few standard products, so affiliates market their messages mainly through standard images and banners, without much content integration.

An important side-effect of performance-based payment as well as context-based selling is that the number of visitors at an affiliate is not a key success criterion in affiliate marketing, meaning that to a marketer an affiliated site that has a clearly defined, active user profile with relatively few visitors can be more valuable than a website with many unfocused visitors. This is because there might be a better match between the end-users and marketer than on the broader website portal. This does not mean that heavy traffic drivers are not valuable in an affiliate marketing network, but the context of the media space has a higher focus than in traditional banner advertising. A product's credibility with consumers increases when a focused site recommends it. Hence, performance can often be higher on a focused website.

Ethics

A consequence of affiliates using context-based selling is that affiliates and marketers both have to consider the ethical issues connected to this. The editorial content of media firms, whether they are websites or print or TV, etc., is often expected by their users to be commercially unbiased, especially when they run articles or stories marked as their own (not clearly marked 'advertisement'). While users have come to expect commercial ads in basically all media, including newspapers, TV and the Internet, they are used to them being separate from the media's own content. Usually, they also expect the media's articles to be written independently of commercial interests. However, there is a grey area. For example, product placement is a technique where products are specifically placed in TV shows and movies where the audience notices them. This technique can be related to context-based selling, in that the advertising forms part of the content. Although this may raise questions from consumers, it can be a significant revenue source for these media (Ebenkamp, 2001).

In a number of situations, both marketers and affiliates are strongly against context-based selling where it misleads the consumer into thinking a marketer's message is actually an unbiased recommendation from the affiliate. No one is interested in getting an image as unethical and untrustworthy. Also, marketers could appear untrustworthy themselves for being related to untrustworthy affiliates. Many affiliates believe their expertise is a key reason why people visit them. If this expertise is compromised, visitors may disappear. On the other hand, many affiliates and marketers do support integrating marketing messages into content, and they definitely do think it is effective (generates higher sales). What is important is that visitors understand that affiliates do have a commercial interest in promoting these products. This does not necessarily negate sales, though. Visitors may regard the fact that the affiliate has chosen to work with a certain marketer as a vote of confidence for that marketer, especially if they trust the affiliate's expertise in that area.

The problem with context-based selling is that is raises serious ethical questions for many people, including the consumers that it is aimed at (Cartellieri et al., 1997). Consumers visiting affiliates may rely on their expertise, particularly the small, specialised websites and communities. If they suspect that an affiliate's articles and recommendations are based on commercial interests, they will probably lose faith in the affiliate. Traditional media (usually) avoid this problem by clearly separating content and advertising. People have learned to take this separation for granted, and may be sceptical towards any integration of editorial content and commercial interests (Donaton, 2000). However, there is some indication that this is changing. For example, Procter & Gamble, one of the world's largest advertisers, in 2001 signed a major advertising deal with media giant Viacom to bundle advertising across a variety of media channels. Among other things, the two companies plan to work together to create content on a TV network. According to an article in the *Wall Street Journal* (Nelson and O'Connell, 2001): 'the bundle could also further blur the line between content and advertising'. Similarly, the growing use of product placement in films and TV can also be seen as a blurring of the lines between advertising and editorial content (Cartellieri et al., 1997; Ebenkamp, 2001).

However, consumers are still sceptical towards this development. At the same time, marketers do not want affiliates to compromise their integrity to sell products (at least not officially), because it can cheapen their own brand if they are associated with what is perceived as unethical marketing. For this reason many affiliates are very wary of using context-based selling. They realise there is a fine line between serving visitors relevant marketing messages at the right time and 'selling out' their credibility. Besides, what can appear fine for one visitor may be unethical for another. There is no clear-cut solution to this problem; it depends on a variety of issues. However, there is definitely a gap between the pure concept and what is actually feasible in practice. As Cartellieri et al. (1997) argue, 'the issue of editorial independence and the possibility of consumer rejection or backlash may ultimately set limits on the pursuit of this approach'.

4.7   END-USER RELATIONS

The end-user is the target of the marketer's marketing and the initial provider of revenues to be split among marketers and affiliates. The more end-users parties in the network have access to, the more revenue potential they have. However, the type of end-users the network has access to is equally important. Hence, the quantity and quality of the potential market of end-users affiliates can provide marketers with is a key determinant of the network's value. Additionally, the issue of customer acquisition comes into effect. Just because there is a potential market, this does not mean that customers are cheap or easy to acquire. As an extension to the issue of customer acquisition comes the question of 'ownership' of these customers – who do they belong to, marketers or affiliates?

Potential Market

Since affiliate marketing requires investments from both marketers and affiliates, in terms of money and learning time, it is critical that they reach enough end-users to have a chance at recouping these investments. Particularly because of the number of affiliates often necessary to make a programme work, marketers may have to spend a lot of time on managing their partners and evaluating results. Affiliate marketing – at least for now – is purely an online affair. This means that consumers are exposed to the programme only while using the Internet. Obviously this means that only people who use the Internet are potential audiences. For example, in Denmark and the UK about a third of the adult population are active Internet users and even in the USA, this figure is only about 40 per cent. In other parts of Europe and most of Asia it is much less (Al-Kibsi et al., 2001). Of the people that use the Internet, the characteristics have broadened over the past few years, but there are still few elderly people using the Internet, and relatively few low-income families (Jupiter Communications, 2000a). This sets boundaries for which types of target groups companies should use affiliate marketing to try and reach. So it is not only a question for marketers of finding the right affiliates to market their products, but also of whether the Internet as a medium is right for reaching the marketer's target groups. While one could argue that there are affiliates for even the smallest niche groups of people, including elderly people, affiliate marketing requires marketers to invest resources in getting established as well as on ongoing maintenance, and most marketers will need a critical mass of affiliates to be able to make enough volume in revenues to recoup these expenses.

Internet marketing as a whole has experienced severe problems over the past couple of years. The effectiveness of banner ads has been unsatisfactory, but no other types of marketing have really been able to take its place. Affiliate marketing attempts to be a more effective alternative to banner advertising, but the fact is that some of the problems associated with banner ads are also present in affiliate marketing. First of all, consumers seem able and willing to resist online ads, even if they do notice them (Bruner et al., 2001).

While the context-based nature of many affiliate marketing ads (written into an affiliate's content) to some degree works against this, consumers still may not be that responsive. Second, people have proved resistant to purchasing online, and have disappointed many (optimistic) estimates. For example, last year AC Nielsen downgraded their estimate of what percentage of purchases will be made online in 2005 by a third – from 30 to 20 per cent (Lindstrom, 2001). Also, online users have proved unwilling to provide information about themselves to the degree predicted by industry experts. Many people hold on to their information sometimes, even if they can get better products or value by releasing it to companies (Hagel and Rayport, 1997). This affects the ability affiliates have to generate leads for marketers.

No matter how much of a win/win situation marketers and affiliates can create amongst themselves, if the volume of purchasing and lead-generation is too low it won't be worth their while. In fact, even though affiliate marketing has been profitable for the firm on a per product basis, once the added overhead costs of running a website, logistics, and allocating employees' time have been added in, it has not reached the overall targets. This shows that profitability has to come from volume as well as positive margins. Affiliate marketing is so dependent on the success of the Internet in general that it will probably never be really successful until enough consumers are willing not only to use it, but also to provide information and perform purchases online. However, almost all surveys and reports stress that this will increasingly happen in the future, although the actual numbers vary.

Customer Acquisition

The theory in much of the Internet marketing literature (e.g. Helmstetter and Metivier, 2000; Lindstrom, 2001; Bruner et al., 2001), and some marketing literature in general (e.g. Peppers and Rogers, 1995; Pine et al., 1995), is that firms should measure the cost of acquiring a new customer versus the future lifetime value of this customer. This means that firms should consider 'investing' in new customers, even if they lose on the initial sale. For example, Amazon.com has publicly acknowledged that it expects to earn $120 per year in revenues on average for each new customer, so it is willing to pay affiliates 15 per cent of revenues for referring customers (Bruner et al., 2001). Even though Amazon.com loses money on the affiliate's sale, because its average margins are less than 15 per cent, it regards this fee as an investment, not just a one-time margin cost. Much research shows that affiliate marketing is the most effective method of acquiring a new customer online (Forrester Research, 1999). Table 4.1 illustrates average customer acquisition costs for six different marketing techniques carried out by buy.com, a large online retailer.

Despite these studies indicating the effectiveness of affiliate marketing in customer acquisition, some marketers have struggled with affiliate marketing programmes. In the Direct Marketing Association's 'State of the Interactive eCommerce Marketing Industry Report 2000: Emerging Trends and Business Practices', online marketers rated affiliate marketing as only a 'somewhat effective' method of attracting new customers (Cotlier, 2001). There are no clear explanations for these differences in effectiveness among marketers, but it may depend on the products or services sold as well as the marketer's ability to be successful, to be active, and to exploit the merits of affiliate marketing.

Table 4.1   An example of customer acquisition costs: buy.com

Media	Cost of acquisition in €	Revenue in € per € spent
Radio	1457	0.07
Print	958	0.10
Public relations	82	1.16
E-mail	24	2.54
Online ads	21	4.61
Affiliates	9	7.15

Source: Azeez (2001). Comments by Gordon Henderson, buy.com's UK Marketing Director

'Ownership'

In principle, many of the customer acquisition surveys looks attractive, because there is indication that gaining a new customer through affiliate marketing is a lot cheaper than banner ads (Forrester Research, 1999). However, the difference is that when someone becomes a customer through a banner ad, he will presumably regard the marketer as the firm who sold him the product and probably go to the marketer's website in the future. On the other hand, when a consumer purchases a product from a marketer through a focused affiliate that he already has a strong relationship with, he may well continue to do this in the future particularly if he trusts that the affiliate's expertise will pick the best offers on products and services that match its audience's needs, perhaps from several different marketers. Naturally this is a critical consideration for marketers when the affiliate's commission becomes a permanent expense in every product sold. Therefore, while the generation of new business can be a win/win situation for affiliates and marketers, however, if not estimated correctly, splitting the revenues from continuous business can become a zero-sum game.

Hence, the question of who the consumer 'belongs to' becomes an issue. With most traditional advertising – and online banner advertising – consumers know that the marketer is selling the products and that the media is only carrying the ads. This procedure is so common that few people question it, and usually the media firm is not held responsible for the purchase (unless it severely overlooks neglect on the advertiser's part). Consumers can easily separate marketer and media. With affiliate marketing, the boundaries between the two are blurred. Affiliates actively market the marketer's products within their own content, and sometimes recommend certain products. If consumers trust the affiliate as a reputable source on its area, they will probably regard the recommendation as trustworthy. Therefore, if they are not satisfied with their purchase, they may hold the affiliate responsible.

Despite this the indistinct ownership, most marketers strongly feel, that they have the full responsibility for consumers' satisfaction with the purchase experience the end-user has. We think this reflects somewhat of an old-fashioned view on the part of marketers. Although they participate in affiliate marketing, they still regard consumers as being 'their' customers. In indicating that they do not think affiliates are responsible for their satisfaction, they downplay affiliates' role in the transaction, for example their expertise and recommendations. Of course, the marketer has the final responsibility of delivering a quality product, but the experience naturally involves much more than the final product. Marketers, many of which have the majority of their advertising in other types of programmes, regard affiliates as passive media, just there to pass on a message. Now this view is not necessarily bad – or good – it just isn't entirely in sync with the affiliate marketing concept. No doubt many affiliates, particularly the hobby sites, are unsophisticated and do not have the professionalism of the larger marketers. However, to gain the advantages of affiliate marketing, marketers need to accept that affiliates have a role to play in the transaction beyond simply passing on a message, and thus also some responsibility to the consumer for their purchase.

Our argument is that the more responsibility an affiliate has to the consumer, the more ownership it has over the relationship with that consumer. Thus if the consumer is dissatisfied, he will complain to the affiliate. Likewise, if he is satisfied, he will be pleased with the affiliate (as well as the marketer). Thus responsibility and ownership are closely linked. The reason marketers do not want to confer responsibility to affiliates is that they want ownership of the consumers that purchase from them (or register their information). Since they usually have the most well-known brand, they believe the consumer wants to rather do business with them, and that they represent better credibility. However, while affiliates may have a less well-known brand, they often have high credibility within the small segment they represent (Forrester Research, 1999). It is not at all certain that consumers who frequent an affiliate's website would rather do business with a marketer than with that affiliate.

The reason that both parties want 'ownership' of the consumer relation is that they can use it to promote and control future purchases. Affiliates are dependent on having this relationship, because it is the basis for their revenues. If consumers feel that they are dealing with the affiliate, rather than the marketer, they will probably keep going back to the affiliate to trade in the future. If consumers feel they are doing business solely with the marketer, they will probably go directly to its website next time they want to buy the same or a similar product. This takes affiliates out of the loop and they do not get revenues. It should be noted affiliates gain higher ownership if they are provided a storefront that they can sell products from (ibid.). This means that they can sell the marketer's products (or collect registrations) without consumers ever leaving their website. In some cases affiliates actually co-brand the storefront, meaning that the products are actually sold under their name as well (ibid.). TradeDoubler lets this solution be a choice for the marketer, but strongly recommends this to be made available for the affiliate. In the USA, there are companies that build 'ready-made' Web stores for e-businesses as an alternative to affiliate marketing programmes, although the methods are not that different (Silverstein, 2001). These companies look to keep customers on a site rather than sending them to another site through an affiliate's link. For example, Affinia helps affiliates build their own stores around specific subject areas or niches. Affinia then 'stocks' the store with items from marketers it services. In early 2000, Affinia claimed to have over one million products available from more than one thousand participating marketers (ibid.). The difference with this approach is that the marketer serves as a 'sub-contractor' to the affiliate, and the affiliate maintains the entire relationship with the end-user, including billing. Most likely the co-branded option will become typical in the future, particularly among larger affiliates with more bargaining power (Forrester Research, 1999).

4.8   NETWORK RELATIONS

Naturally, participants regard the size of the affiliate marketing network as a major advantage, because it gave them instant access to a large number of potential partners. Particularly marketers find it valuable that shortly after starting a new programme they can have hundreds or even thousands of affiliate applicants. Additionally, the characteristics of the ongoing relations can be valuable, particularly the adaptability and contractual flexibility.

Network Access

The large affiliate marketing brokers have literally hundreds of thousands or even millions of affiliates in their network (Helmstetter and Metivier, 2000). This means that a new marketer very quickly has an opportunity to form many partnerships with affiliates. Just joining the programme has some value to marketers, since there is already a critical mass of potential partners. In a way, previous marketers have served as trailblazers who helped bring in affiliates to the programme, which new marketers now can gain from. The first marketers that joined could expect few affiliates, but now there are thousands of new affiliates signing up in Europe each week. Broad distribution of points of sale is often perceived as a valuable prospect for marketers in an affiliate marketing network.

However, in more recent literature there has been criticism of the concept of marketers simply getting as many affiliates as possible (e.g. Bruner et al., 2001). As explained previously, the reason for this is that too many unfocused affiliates can dilute a marketer's brand, and they also require administration and communications, even though much of this is automated. This points out that particularly marketers are not overly enthusiastic about a large number of potential affiliates. For example, some B2B marketers reject 90 per cent of affiliate applicants because their characteristics and profile do not harmonise with their marketing strategy. Affiliates are more interested in having more marketers to choose from, presumably because there are relatively few to choose from. The overall conclusion on the value of network access in our opinion is that quantity is valuable up to a certain point, which has probably been reached in terms of affiliates for the large networks. However, the quality of potential partners is also a determinant of value, no matter how large the network is. With regards to this quality, the number of potential partners is so large that the affiliate base presumably reflects the general characteristics of online media/websites. The quality is there; marketers just need the right tools to locate it in relation to their specific needs. This may indicate a need for the broker to actively match affiliates and marketers based on their knowledge of the network.

Contractual Flexibility

As mentioned previously, the performance of an affiliate–marketer relationship usually improves over time. This is because there is a learning and adaptation process involved. Over time, as performance improves, the relationship becomes valuable to both parties. Marketers are dependent on affiliates to reach the ultimate consumers of their products and services, and affiliates are dependent on marketers for revenues. In investing time in building up the performance of the partnership, they increase the future revenues they can expect to generate. While marketers usually have no reason to end a relationship with an affiliate, since the payment is performance-based, it can happen. For example, if the marketer decides to change its strategy and stop or cut back on affiliate marketing, this would affect its affiliates. An even more serious example happened in TradeDoubler's network when BOL, the online arm of Bertelsmann, decided to discontinue its online presence in Denmark, and thus end its relationships with all affiliates. This left thousands of Danish affiliates with bookstores, recommendations, and links to the BOL website on their websites, but with nothing on the other end. Almost from one day to the next, their revenue stream ended. These affiliates have all spent time searching the BOL website for appropriate books for their customers, writing book recommendations and even putting in links into their actual content. Thus not only do they lose their revenue stream, but they lose all the time put into their investment. Hence, the contractual flexibility that is an integral part of performance-based payment, as explained earlier, can have significantly negative consequences.

However, marketers and affiliates do not necessarily perceive it negatively. Both parties highly value their freedom and flexibility, in particularly marketers. Naturally, since there is no time limit on an affiliate marketing relationship, both parties have the option to end it if they are dissatisfied or want to change direction. Setting a three-month warning period could be an option, but the parties do not seem to want it. Perhaps if enough BOL-type episodes occur, affiliates will think differently. Marketers are less at risk because of the high number of affiliates they have. Affiliates do sometimes change marketers to match and update the content of their sites. However, the high number of affiliates ensures that marketers always will have many affiliates, given a typical probability distribution.

Another consequence of this flexibility is that marketers can change their payment structure with affiliates when they want. Research suggests that marketers should vary their payment structure for affiliates, in order to keep the best performing affiliates loyal (Jupiter Communications, 1998b). Particularly if affiliates are compensated for clicks, marketers should make sure that those with higher conversion rates to purchases are compensated with higher commissions (ibid.). As noted earlier, 15 per cent of affiliates typically generate at least 80 per cent of sales (ibid.), making it important to keep these affiliates loyal in order to maintain the necessary volume to cover fixed costs. Thus, marketers should offer affiliates different solutions depending on their previous performance.

The matrix in Figure 4.1 illustrates how the commission structure to the affiliate can vary depending on the conversion rate from unique visitor to actual sales. Thus, the segmentation of affiliates is also performance-based, and not based on number of visitors alone. For example, in segment 2 of the matrix, the websites are defined by driving a conversion rate between 1–3 per cent, and each sale costs the advertiser between €7 and €15, which of course must be compared to the profit margin on the specific product.[1] In segment 1 the cost of a sale will never exceed €15, and in segment 3 the cost will never exceed €2.50. In this example the lead is not included in the calculation, as a lead often has an isolated value.

Unique visitors, leads and sales that are broken into tailored solutions on the marketers' website define the key success criteria. A lead could be that visitors type in their data or ask for further information. Hence, it is possible to define multiple leads, and the value can differentiate among these.

Possible distribution of affiliates		Click (€)	Lead1 (€)	Lead2 (€)	Sale (€)	Conversion rate from click to sale (%)
10%	Segment 1	0.20	0.60	0.90	2.50	+3
30%	Segment 2	0.15	0.50	0.75	2.50	1–3
60%	Segment 3	0	0.40	0.60	2.50	0–1

Figure 4.1   Performance-based segmentation of affiliates

Similarly, the commission on sales can vary depending on products and the order sum, so marketers can take profit margins into consideration. This segmentation principle is somewhat comparable to how airlines segment their travellers into Gold and Silver cardholders based on their previous travelling patterns, and reward them accordingly, only affiliate marketing segments and rewards the media, not the actual end-user.

4.9   CHAPTER CONCLUSION

Affiliate marketing is potentially attractive to firms because of the value it provides for its participants. Eight key resources, each of which are created during the interactions between participants and/or exchanged among them, drive this value.

Participants can gain value from being associated with a partner with a strong brand, thus improving their own credibility with end-users. However, this can also go the other way and untrustworthy partners can harm a participant's brand. Additionally, participating in affiliate marketing can give marketers branding/awareness that they would have to pay affiliates for in other types of marketing methods. Although affiliates would like payment for branding, marketers have the power to reject paying them for it.

Consequently, affiliate marketing is not useful for brand awareness or brand building, but rather brand association, where credibility, trust and commitment are of high importance.

Performance-based payment is valuable to participants because it aligns the interests of affiliates and marketers, thus giving affiliates an incentive to invest in marketers' success for the long-term benefit of both parties. The payment structure also allows marketers to shift some of their performance risk to affiliates, which gives marketers much better accountability, but makes it much more difficult for affiliates to budget future revenues. Finally, the payment structure shifts the initiative to affiliates, by decentralising the process of monitoring advertising performance and optimising results. This decentralising increases decision-making units in the network and improves learning.

The tracking technology makes performance-based payment possible, and it makes communications and administration more efficient, particularly for marketers with thousands of affiliates. The technology builds on the Internet, which connects parties, making it possible for them to transfer users. Moreover, once the technology is developed additional parties can be added to the network at very little cost.

Participants gain value from the fact that many niche affiliates have a lot of information on their audience, which they can use to improve performance. Furthermore, affiliates have access to ongoing performance statistics that they can use to adjust the messages they present their users in order to maximise performance.

An important characteristic of a many-to-many affiliate marketing network is that participants have a neutral third party to measure and verify their performance. This brokerage gives participants the trust in each other necessary to invest in long-term relationships.

In order to maximise performance, affiliates seek to select those marketers and/or products that are most relevant to their users. Many of them integrate marketing messages in their content in the form of links or images, which attract significantly higher conversion rates than banner ads. However, affiliates run the risk of their users perceiving them as being unethical, and thus going elsewhere for information and recommendations.

Marketers gain access to a large population of potential customers through affiliates, to whom they can market their products and services. However, in most countries this is still a minority of the total population. Additionally, online users have been reluctant to purchase online and even to submit information, a fact that limits the volume a marketer can hope to gain from affiliate marketing. Regarding the customers that can be gained online, affiliate marketing appears to be one of the cheapest methods of acquiring them. However, as opposed to most other marketing methods, marketers run the risk with affiliate marketing that affiliates retain 'ownership' of these customers and thus continue to reap revenues from them. In the future, joint ownership of customers will probably become more common.

Participants gain access to a large number of potential partners when joining the network, particularly marketers. However, this is not valued so highly, mainly because too many partners are costly and can dilute a firm's brand. Participants find it valuable that they can terminate a partnership when they want if they are dissatisfied. Both parties appreciate that marketers can differentiate among affiliates and reward those that perform best with higher commissions.

NOTE

1. This cost is calculated as follows:
    $(100 \cdot$ click commission + sales commission $\cdot$ (conversion rate/100))/(conversion rate $\cdot$ 100)

PART III

Strategic Considerations

Strategic Considerations

Affiliate marketing is growing to the point where it is becoming interesting to firms involved in online activity, whether they sell and market products, or they provide information and content. Basically, the way firms can enter into affiliate marketing could be classified by means of two different strategic modes. These two modes (Mintzberg et al., 1998) are:

- Deliberate. Affiliate marketing is evaluated at top management level and considered as an important strategic tool for the firm. If chosen, its use is formulated through a central plan.
- Emergent. Affiliate marketing starts out at a lower level in the firm, and if effective may spread to other departments.

According to Mintzberg et al. (1998), this distinction can be made for a firm's strategy or strategic initiatives, insofar as they are defined as a pattern or consistency in action. The distinction is applicable to both affiliates and marketers. However, for small firms there is not much difference as 'top management' makes most decisions, particularly the many small homepages. They can still start by testing affiliate marketing on a limited scale, though, and broaden it if it proves successful.

In the planned approach, top management holds affiliate marketing up against the firm's strategic objectives and determines whether it can help achieve them. They need to evaluate the potential benefits and drawbacks of affiliate marketing (described in the previous chapter), in relation to their own needs and requirements. When done, they design a specific strategy for their participation, along with implementation guidelines. Critical questions are:

- How does affiliate marketing fit in with our overall strategic objectives?
- What benefits can affiliate marketing offer our firm specifically?
- What requirements does affiliate marketing put on our firm?
- What are the critical success factors for us to succeed with affiliate marketing?

The planned approach has so far been typical for the vast majority of marketers in TradeDoubler's network, much more so than for affiliates. The reason for this is that TradeDoubler charges an initial set-up fee per country, regardless of how much the firm uses the programme, so it is unlikely that a single department or product manager would find it desirable to fund this expense, without planning and an estimation of the potential of entering into an affiliate marketing network. However, there have been several cases with multinational firms where management in a single country have decided to enter into affiliate marketing, and later on the firm's management in other countries have seen the benefits and joined in. In any case, TradeDoubler typically goes through a sales process lasting several weeks or months before a marketer decides to join, only after long and intensive considerations. With the set-up fee and monthly fees to TradeDoubler, a marketer would expect to spend a minimum of €20,000 in its first year of affiliate marketing, even if the programme is a failure. Besides the money issue, there are also other considerations associated with entering affiliate marketing, which may require a top-management decision. We get into these problems later on. However, very large companies may make the decision on the divisional or departmental level. This has been the case with TDC and Orange, which have entered TradeDoubler's Danish network only with certain parts of their companies. Mobilix' business division, for example, has chosen to begin affiliate marketing on its own accord (without participation from its private customer division).

The emergent approach, on the other hand, is characterised by a 'learning by doing' process, where firms gradually test out different aspects of affiliate marketing, and keep them if they prove successful (Mintzberg et al., 1998). This can be seen as an incremental approach. Strategy slowly builds over time as knowledge is gained. Since joining the network is free for affiliates, they are much more likely to adopt this approach. In particular, the larger 'conglomerate' media companies like TV2, Metropol, Bonnier, TVDanmark or Aller Press, all in Denmark, may start by attempting to use affiliate marketing in one segment of their website(s).

While we recognise the viability of the emergent approach, we adopt the perspective of the deliberate approach in the following two chapters. We do this because it allows us to develop a standard process description, something that would be difficult given the 'messiness' of an emergent approach (Mintzberg et al., 1998). Finally, as mentioned previously, the minimum of resources required for marketers to participate almost guarantees that they will apply, at least some extent, a rather deliberate approach. Marketers face the majority of considerations, and are covered most extensively in Chapter 6.

In the following two chapters, we address the strategic considerations and frequent problems that most often occur for firms considering getting into affiliate marketing. Because of the different roles affiliates and marketers play they face different issues, so we address each group in turn, affiliates in Chapter 5, and marketers in Chapter 6. We utilise a basic framework of three levels of strategy – corporate, business and operational (Johnson and Scholes, 1999) to structure the process. It should be noted that in practice these levels overlap, and the process is less structured. We first examine how a firm's key corporate and business level objectives affect its potential use of affiliate marketing, and identify the main problems they typically face. It is at this level a firm typically decides whether or not to adopt affiliate marketing. We then present an analysis of the key operational issues firms have to address if they decide for it. This includes the resource requirements and tasks necessary. In Chapter 6, for marketers specifically, we identify four different options for adoption, and explain why each option is relevant and what it requires. We finalise Part III by bringing together Chapters 3 to 6 and present an explanation model in Chapter 7 that identifies specific ties between the various roles, considerations and value elements firms can expect as part of an affiliate marketing network.

5. Affiliate Considerations

5.1 AFFILIATE CONSIDERATIONS – CORPORATE AND BUSINESS LEVEL

The affiliate as a media firm usually has two general ambitions – to deliver content to its users, and to generate revenues (Bruner et al., 2001). For some affiliates, affiliate marketing allows them to potentially increase the value of their content, by providing users with a place where they know they can find good products/marketers (Helmstetter and Metivier, 2000) or actually implementing interactive micro-sites made available by marketers, thereby creating additional and content-based functionalities on its own website. However, the most important benefit of affiliate marketing for affiliates is that it gives them an opportunity to potentially increase their revenues (Helmstetter and Metivier, 2000; Bruner et al., 2001). There are four basic ways to generate revenue from a content-based website: subscriptions, advertising, content syndication, and affiliate commissions (Barsh et al., 2001). For the majority of these websites, subscriptions and content syndication generate very little, if any, revenue (Barsh et al., 2001). Regarding advertising revenues, the prices of banner advertising have fallen drastically recently (Sommer, 2001), and many of these firms are desperately looking for other sources of revenues.

While affiliate marketing in principle does seem attractive for many potential affiliates, many of them have been reluctant to get involved, while they were still able to use banner advertising. However, now that this option is getting less attractive, affiliate marketing is becoming relatively more attractive. Perhaps for the wrong reasons, though, as affiliate marketing should to some degree complement impression-based advertising, rather than substitute for it (IDC, 1999). In any case, there are still some problems that need to be considered. TradeDoubler's experience has shown that potential affiliates, particularly the larger ones, face a major problem in determining the viability and attractiveness of affiliate marketing for them specifically – they often fear that their 'objectivity' will be compromised if they mix editorial and commercial references.

Viability of Commercialised Content

Affiliates have a profile, which they have developed over time. This profile reflects the firm's characteristics, which typically cover its content type, target audience and ethics. Media firms use their profile as a way to differentiate and position themselves among potential users. According to Forrester Research (1999): 'media companies invest heavily over a number of years to build an audience, understand its interests, and develop content that meets those needs'. Particularly on the Internet, where anyone, in principle, can publish content, a well-respected media profile that carries credibility with users is a valuable commodity (Forrester Research, 1999). The stamp of credibility and trustworthiness often takes a long time to build. Thus, media firms are very wary of any initiative that may harm their credibility and/or dilute their profile. A traditional hindrance that is met from the big media is the fact that affiliate marketing is content-related and most newspapers and other editorial-oriented websites are afraid to mix editorial and commercial references.

Many newspapers and other editorial websites are somewhat resistant to integrating commercial links into their articles and other contents. They believe that users count on their editorial content being free of commercial interests, and that mixing the two will lessen the value of their content. To some degree this is true, however, it depends on the profile of the media. Political and news media are more dependent on a commercial-free editorial process than entertainment media, and the line between news and advertising is still considered sacrosanct (Donaton, 2000). However, with entertainment and advertising the line has become increasingly blurred. This resistance is somewhat similar to the same process TV and film have been going through (mainly in the USA) when they started to include product placement in their shows, where the discussion concerned reliability and objectiveness, free of influence from sponsors (Ebenkamp, 2001). In fact, there are still sometimes very strong protests against integration of commercial interests and editorial content in traditional media, typically focusing on the 'manipulation' of viewers.

Product placement in movies has existed for many years, but is far from fully accepted by everyone, even in the USA (Ebenkamp, 2001; Donaton, 2000). With affiliate marketing, the sponsors have the opportunity to be integrated even further into the context, and the barriers are pushed a little further, again with many objections from different parties. For example, the American Society for Newspaper Editions and the Online News Association have called on both advertisers and publishers to agree to guidelines protecting the dividing line between advertising and editorial (Kavanagh, 1999).

There are political considerations inside the company as well as readers to satisfy, and for certain media firms it may be best not to use context-based selling at all. Media companies should definitely make sure they know how their readers and editorial staff will respond to this, and if in doubt could consider very gradually testing it in less critical parts of the website. Even the newspapers and magazines that are prepared to use affiliate marketing have problems with integrating the links into the editorial matter. Because of conflicts with the editors, many newspapers and magazines decline the opportunity of an additional revenue-driver available just by integrating the marketers' links into the editorial context, at the most they link to marketers in their newsletters distributed by e-mail, but not on their website.

However, affiliate marketing is not infeasible for editorial sites, but it depends on the user's relation to the website. A newspaper that writes a book review, for example, might as well link up to the place where the reader can either get more information or actually buy the book, whether or not the review positively recommends the book or not. If readers can see that the affiliate does not hold back punches and is critical of books when necessary, they may accept this. There exist many examples of editorial sites, which are focused on providing content for their specific communities, that integrate affiliate marketing links into their content and they manage to sustain an essentially non-commercial profile. Hence, there are some political considerations that content-based websites must make when engaging in affiliate marketing. They must also remember that visitors to content sites go there mainly to seek information, not commerce (Barsh et al., 2001).

It can be argued that it is not affiliate marketing as such that is in an immature stage, but rather that some media have not yet been willing to establish regular use of it. However, many media apply both affiliate links and impression banners. In any case, media companies that do use affiliate marketing should at least consider the need to develop some type of context-based selling approach, such as integrating links into articles and other text. Otherwise, they are simply showing banners, and will probably not achieve a high enough performance to justify the budgeting uncertainty of using affiliate marketing over impression-based advertising. Then again, it should be noted that the majority of websites are not news-delivering sites, but entertainment or 'information' websites, where context-based selling is feasible for many, given that users are informed of the commercial interests and believe that editorial interests are not compromised.

5.2   AFFILIATE CONSIDERATIONS – OPERATIONAL LEVEL

Affiliate marketing does not affect an affiliate's operations to the same degree as a marketer's, but there are certain issues that need to be considered. We have identified two main issues that affiliates have to address specifically as a result of adopting affiliate marketing. These are:

- An increased amount of activities relative to the requirements of banner advertising (where everything is outsourced). The inherent learning and long-term adoption that makes affiliate marketing attractive requires affiliates to devote resources to various activities.
- A more elaborate budgeting process. The increased uncertainty of performance-based payment requires skilful budgeting and performance analysis.

It should be noted that participation in affiliate marketing for affiliates does not actually demand that any of this is done. Since affiliates are responsible for their own performance, they can just place a link on their site and nothing else. But if they want to be successful, and especially if they are professional websites that have to optimise capacity and generate certain revenue to survive, managing these issues are important for their success. We cover each of the two issues in turn, describing their requirements and operational consequences for the affiliate.

Increased Activities

With traditional banner advertising, the implementation and other functionalities are handled either by the website's media agency or the banner network. However, with affiliate marketing the website needs to be closely involved in the implementation processes. Thus, a website's initial consideration, with regard to becoming an affiliate, is to examine what requirements affiliate marketing brings, and how it can achieve them. Hereafter, the potential affiliate must determine whether it is possible to carry this out with regard to its existing set-up.

With advertising banner networks, media firms have been used to not having to implement the actual banners as the banner networks have handled this. This has been possible because of standardised banner formats that the banner networks have easily implemented on specific places on the websites. However, with affiliate marketing and content-related links, there is a need for flexible solutions, and in order for the linking to be successful, implementation is not a procedure the media should outsource to a third party.

The reason for this is that affiliates, in order to be successful, need to have an ongoing learning process in which they continuously monitor their performance and adjust their links and banners to achieve the best results. Similarly, text links that are integrated into the affiliate's content cannot readily be done by a media agency because of the lack of standardisation.

Even though there are manageable procedures for implementing leads on the affiliates' websites, they now have to actively take part in this implementation, which they are not used to from traditional banner advertisement. Thus, the very flexibility that can make affiliate marketing a high-performance initiative for media firms also demands of them increased attention, longer implementation time and additional resources. According to a TradeDoubler employee: 'Especially the big media are not used to spending time on implementing different links. We make the links easily accessible, and it is very easily implemented, but the affiliate must make it a routine to implement links'. She further states, that: 'often when we work with a large client, we spend a lot of time teaching them how to implement the links even though it is a very simple process that takes less than 2 minutes (per link), which we have explained thoroughly on our website'. The solution to this problem is that affiliates must be willing to allocate resources, not only to implement links and banners, but also to test new variations on a regular basis. This does not require specialised computer skills, since the process is fairly simple and standardised, and TradeDoubler explains it in detail. Naturally, these resources are an investment, but they are fairly modest and existing personnel can handle the task with a few hours a week (depending on the number of links and banners the affiliate has). These resources do not so much cover the implementation of links and banners, as they cover the testing and evaluation of results from different variations of links and banners. Successful affiliates invest in building the learning necessary to generate high performance in the long term, and to maintain it even as circumstances change (for example if marketers change products or drop out completely).

Budgeting

One of the drawbacks of affiliate marketing for affiliates is the uncertainty of not being able to budget with specific advertising revenues ahead of time. As we described in Chapter 4, some of the risk is shifted from marketer to affiliate. One of the immediate concerns of the big media is that it is not easy to calculate and budget with a performance-based income, until they have had actual experience with affiliate marketing revenue streams.

With the small hobby websites that have never had any revenue before, it may not be such a big problem, but for the professional media that have people hired and are used to generating their revenues through banner advertising, it is a problem. However, this is just a problem affiliates may have to learn to address. Work by Forrester Research (2001) indicates that 82 per cent of online advertising will be at least partially performance-based by 2003.

Most professional websites and online communities have relied on income from advertising, and they have been used to selling banner space on the websites in accordance with offline principles, where the number of visitors/impressions and demographic segmentation work as the success criteria for placing an ad. However, with the enabling of interactive and tracking opportunities for online media, more and more action- and behaviour-oriented success criteria have gradually been introduced to online marketing. As described previously, there are four types of transaction from which the online media can generate an income: payment per impression, per click, per lead, and per sale.

With payments per impression the marketer's aim is to build awareness, and the website's budgeting is based on a capacity calculation of how many visitors visit their website over how long a period of time, and how much space they can dedicate to banner ads on their page(s). With this information it is fairly easy to estimate an income, which again allows the media to plan for developments and other activities on the website. This is the advantage of CPM banner advertising, which is impression-based payment, because the media's risk is reduced.

Click-based payment is the first level of performance-based payments, which depends on an action from the user. Hence the incentive for the affiliate/media to create a content-related link whether it is a banner ad or a simple text link, is higher, as it can be assumed that a click is caused by an interest on the part of the user, which is triggered from the environment the user is in when exposed to the link. The website should be able to charge a significantly higher payment per click than per impression, because the user actively acknowledges an interest in the marketer's message. A text link that is integrated in the content may not generate the same awareness that the banner does, but the banner will typically not generate the same interest for the user as the content-related text link. Thus different measures must be calculated into the media's budget as the market prices for impressions, clicks, leads, and sales vary according to placements and objectives.

It should be noted that the reason marketers in affiliate networks pay lower costs per click is because they have other payment structures as well, thus offering the media a variety of income generators. If they pay for clicks, they also pay for either leads or sales as well. An affiliate gets payment for all the action a user takes, so it only gets paid for a click if the users do not generate a lead or buy anything. Hence, it is only natural that click payments are lower in long-term affiliate marketing relations compared to short-term banner campaigns, where the marketing objective often is awareness rather than actions, and they do not measure beyond click-through or simple leads. For short-term campaigns, the click payment must cover the possibility of a lead or sale as well. Nevertheless, it is still possible for the affiliate/media to make a rough estimation on a conversion rate and calculate an approximate income, similarly to the principles of impression.

Lead payments appear to be regarded as the type of performance-based payments that are best for both parties; because the media delivers a potential client from a community that it assumes to be valuable to the marketer. At the same time the marketer is responsible for the actual sale, which the affiliate has no direct influence on. In general there is some agreement between both parties that the role of an affiliate is to bring the user up to a lead (e.g. a registration), and that the marketer's role is to convert the lead to an actual sale.

Payments for leads depend on the users' actions on the website they are directed to via a link, and in the short run it is very difficult for the media to calculate income opportunities on actual actions. This means that the media to some degree must consider it as an additional value to be able to direct its users to another website where the user can and will get other opportunities than on the affiliate's website. Because the income opportunities are not easily calculated, but they depend on a closer relationship where the affiliate actually recommends the user to visit the marketer's site, the media and the marketer must be willing to enter a long-term interdependent relationship different from a campaign-oriented marketer–media set-up.

Payments for generated sales are, in principle, similar to payment per lead. However, the sales function opens up the opportunity for the media to start acting as a reseller. In research reports and articles from the USA there are many examples where online media have build a marketplace or specific product stores, where, via product links or store fronts made available by the marketer, they can start offering products they see as valuable for their community (Forrester Research, 1999; IDC, 1999). This way the media rely on the purchasing behaviour of their visitors/community, and their own ability to promote and select the appropriate products, similar to the considerations resellers have when arranging in-store promotions and utility of shelf space. This integration of content doesn't take space and income capacity from awareness-oriented banners, so the media can simultaneously sell banner spaces with awareness objectives at different prices.

Consequently, affiliate marketing mainly generates income via integrated links and not short-term banner campaigns, emphasising long-term relationships. This integration of commercial links demands that media firms start thinking like offline resellers, optimising the use of 'shelf space'. Even if a media firm and marketer arrange a short period of exposure via banner ads, they must differentiate the principles of awareness building, where the marketer pays per impressions, and relationship building, where the marketer pays per action. It is not obvious which method can generate the highest income for the media, but they must be aware of the different uses, and that the two systems, campaign banners and affiliate links, complement rather than cannibalise each other.

6. Marketer Considerations

6.1 MARKETER CONSIDERATIONS – CORPORATE AND BUSINESS LEVEL

A potential marketer has two considerations before entering an affiliate network. Does it fit into the vision and strategic objectives? And what are the functional consequences? Since affiliate marketing requires quite a large investment from marketers during the first year, only firms that have the Internet as an important part of their strategy will typically consider it. Furthermore, as described earlier, some products and services have so far proven much more successful than others in affiliate marketing. Thus marketers selling high-involvement products may not be as successful (IDC, 1999). It should be noted, though, that marketers can still use affiliate marketing to generate leads on potential customers that they can follow up on offline. Seen even more broadly, affiliate marketing can be a medium for the marketer to reach all of its interest groups; these are typically potential customers and employees, but it could in principle be any interest group, as long as they can be reached via the Internet. This basically covers all interest groups (e.g. investors, the public, suppliers), it only influences the character of the affiliate network and the resources spent on developing and retaining the network. However, as we have mentioned before, the expenses for a marketer of participating in affiliate marketing delimits the types of interest groups it pays to reach. Therefore, potential customers are almost always the interest group that is targeted.

Affiliate marketing is not only a strategic decision concerning sales and marketing, it is also a political decision with the company and its stakeholders, whether it decides to become active in a different set-up, where the media/reseller/affiliate needs to take an active part in order to be successful. In order to do this the company must use resources to continuously motivate, educate and communicate to affiliates on different levels, similar to how companies administer various offline distribution channels.

Marketers have different purposes for having an online presence, thus there are various messages to communicate and various interest groups to reach via affiliate marketing. The simplest form of affiliate marketing is to reach end-users in the environment they are in when searching for information on the Internet. This B2C ('business to consumer') orientation is mainly related to those products and services that are feasible to sell and/or market on the Internet. The development of people's buying habits and general Internet usage patterns must also be taken into consideration when starting an affiliate marketing programme with a B2C focus. In any case, having a B2C focus often relates to using affiliate marketing to reach as many people as possible, within the basic target markets set up.

B2B (business to business) is often quite different from B2C, though (Gehman, 2001a). Businesses that sell to other businesses can more easily identify potential customers ahead of time than B2C marketers, and they are typically more focused in their marketing efforts. This is also the case with affiliate marketing. In B2B affiliate marketing there are two typical set-ups; one that takes in the online resellers as affiliates, and one that takes in the clients/potential clients as affiliates, who then make the purchases via a link or a storefront on their own sites or intranet, thus establishing an extranet. A third B2B affiliate set-up is more focused on a pull strategy, where companies do not try to push the products through the online distribution systems, either because of legal restrictions or because the product is not well suited for distribution on the Internet. The strategy behind this set-up can be compared to traditional PR, and an example could be the pharmaceutical industry, where firms are restricted to selling their products via certified offline outlets. However, many users search for health-related information on the Internet, where it would be relevant for pharmaceutical companies to, for example, offer subscriptions to their newsletters, and this way educate and influence users' decisions.

In general there exist two main problems associated with affiliate marketing that potential marketers need to address:

- Marketers with traditional offline resellers run the risk that these resellers perceive affiliate marketing to be a threat to them, sometimes resulting in a channel conflict.
- Marketers find it difficult to 'control' their marketing and their brand, due to the large number of potential affiliates.

We address each of these problems in turn.

Resellers

Affiliate marketing is still a relatively new concept and it has mainly been focused towards online consumer products like travel, books, CDs, consumer electronics, and financial services. Marketers selling these products often have a consumer focus (B2C). In order to expand the concept into more industrial products and services (B2B), the traditional form of affiliate marketing must be modified and adapted for several reasons. Most importantly, many of these types of firms have existing resellers that sell their products offline.

When a firm with existing resellers becomes engaged in affiliate marketing, there are several political and strategic considerations to pay attention to with regard to the firm's end-user and reseller relations, and how deeply the affiliate marketing programme needs to be integrated into the firm's organisation and its established associations. Many industrially oriented companies are path-dependent because of relationships that are established over long periods of time (Håkansson and Snehota, 1995), which are, and probably will continue to be, a foundation for daily sales and distributions. The problem is that existing resellers can feel threatened by affiliate marketing, because they are taken out of the loop in the marketer's Internet strategy. Resellers often invest time and resources in building a marketer's business, and thus want to gain from this over time. There have been many examples of retailers threatening to stop selling marketer's products altogether if they start selling products online (Lindstrom, 2001).

In order to avoid channel conflicts, it is important that affiliate marketing brokers are able to offer solutions where marketers can treat their strategic partners/resellers more favourably than a 'random affiliate', still keep control over their distribution, and at the same time provide the different affiliates with incentives to be part of an affiliate marketing programme. This problem is not only relevant for affiliate marketing, but for any firm that wants to move some of its business online where channel conflicts can arise (Lindstrom, 2001). There is no easy solution, and many firms facing this problem have handled it differently. Avoiding channel conflict can be done if a firm makes sure intermediaries/resellers are not competing for the same end-users under the same circumstances. It is important to avoid cannibalising revenues and profits from existing channels (Bucklin et al., 1996).

Because of more integrated processes and higher interdependencies in B2B relationships than in B2C relationships, it is vital for a B2B company to involve its existing resellers in the affiliate marketing programme, which requires a modified model that goes beyond traditional affiliate marketing. Later in this chapter, we suggest various affiliate marketing options, where we specifically consider how some of them take existing resellers into consideration.

Lack of Control

It is often a major deterrent for firms that they feel they lose control of their marketing and brand in an affiliate marketing network (Cotlier, 2001), because they do not have the resources to monitor all their affiliates. First and foremost, marketers are scared that their brand can become diluted if it is exposed too widely and unfocused through a large number of affiliates. Second, marketers run the risk of moral hazard (Jacobides and Croson, 2001), which can occur if it is in the affiliates' interest to try and cheat the marketer. For example, an opportunistic affiliate may oversell a marketer's product or even lie about it to get a sale, and when the user complains, it is the marketer's responsibility. To minimise these risks, firms have the option of setting strategies for exactly which type of affiliates they want, and to remove some on an ongoing basis if they do not live up to expectations. As we mentioned earlier, a key characteristic of the 'pure' affiliate marketing concept is that affiliates control much of the partnership, through a 'bottom-up' type of selection. However, for companies that have a very well guarded brand, the advantages that come out of this may not be worth the risk of having their brand misrepresented. For these companies, they are still willing to participate in affiliate marketing, but only if they are certain that they can tightly control their partnerships. In cases where the marketer is very brand sensitive, they often reject more than 90 per cent of the affiliates that apply to join, because the firm feels that they would dilute its brand. This stands in contrast to many other marketers, who are happy to get as many affiliates as possible, which basically means more marketing channels.

The solution is in part to set up measures that allow marketers more control of their relationships, if they want it. Naturally, affiliates must know these terms in advance so they can choose whether to sign up or not. For example, marketers can spend resources actively recruiting the affiliates they want, and sorting out those they are not sure of. Also, they can spend resources monitoring whether affiliates live up to their standards. These measures require resources, and will always have their limitations.

6.2 MARKETER CONSIDERATIONS – OPERATIONAL LEVEL

Depending on how a marketer decides to use affiliate marketing, we have identified four basic set-ups that can be implemented:

1. Using affiliate marketing strictly as another channel for marketing. This option simply measures the performance of affiliates and pays them

accordingly. There is little integration with the rest of the marketer's organisation.

2. Using affiliate marketing for generating leads as well as sales. This option passes on leads generated by affiliates to other parts of the organisation that actively follow up on them.
3. Fully integrating affiliate marketing into the company. This option connects the firm's logistics system to the affiliate marketing process.
4. Utilising a reverse model of affiliate marketing. This option stretches the traditional concept to allow for a set-up that involves the marketer's existing resellers.

Through our research we have identified these four options, with which a marketer can engage in affiliate marketing. They are listed in terms of complexity for the marketer. The more complex the solution is, the more it requires of the marketer's organisation in terms of resources. However, the more complex solutions are often more productive in the long run, and take into consideration barriers that otherwise would prevent the marketer from using affiliate marketing.

When a marketer uses affiliate marketing programmes strictly for marketing purposes, the operational considerations are related to traditional marketing planning tools, the marketing mix, budgeting, and marketing information systems. When a marketer uses affiliate marketing as a lead and sale generator, resources from the sales team and call centres must be allocated in order to make use of the leads generated via the programme and affiliate marketing becomes an integrated part of the marketer's CRM system. When a marketer decides to fully integrate its affiliate marketing programme, there is a need for a corporate solution with co-branded interfaces and a completely tailored set-up, so the firm can plan and manage production and logistics in correspondence with sales and leads generated via the affiliate marketing programme, hence, making the programme a part of its ERP system. The reason why marketers engage in a reverse affiliation model also stems from a need to secure its distribution channels, and to avoid channel conflicts. In this case, the initiator of the programme becomes the channel/affiliate that directs leads and sales to its resellers. In the following, we illustrate the benefits and drawbacks of each of these options, and explain in which situations they are applicable. We finish off with an examination of the resource requirements for each option held up against each other.

Affiliate Marketing as a Marketing Channel

When affiliate marketing is applied simply as a marketing channel, there is little integration with the marketer's existing organisation. Affiliate marketing serves as an extra, isolated marketing channel. It is important to note that affiliate marketing is only one of many marketing methods and should therefore be seen in relation to marketers' other marketing activities. Figure 6.1 illustrates various marketing methods according to their cost of advertising and reach, where affiliate marketing is seen as low-cost advertising with low reach.

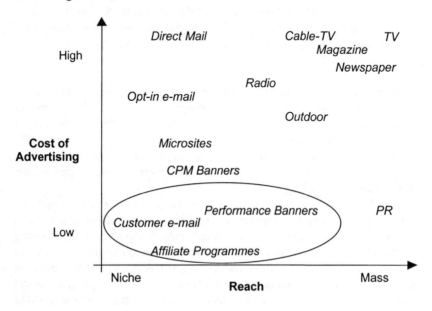

Figure 6.1   Affiliate marketing's place in the media mix

As illustrated in the figure, affiliate marketing should be used mainly as a tool to reach niche segments, rather than for mass marketing. Additionally, the fact that it is relatively low-cost means that it can be applied as an ongoing initiative, rather than a short-term campaign-based initiative. Hence, affiliate marketing should be considered an underlying marketing tool that is constantly active and that can support campaigns and other marketing initiatives throughout the year. As mentioned previously, much of the value in affiliate marketing lies in building long-term learning relationships with affiliates, meaning that a long-term strategy is needed. However, the marketer can be more or less active in the affiliate marketing network according to seasonal activities, and other initiatives like new product introductions.

In order to make an affiliate marketing programme a success, it is important that marketers assist the broker in recruiting a valuable affiliate network and exploiting the potential of the network. When recruiting affiliates, the marketer must plan initiatives and offer incentives for affiliates to enter the network. Once potential affiliates are exposed to the affiliate marketing programme, either from the marketer's own website or via the broker, it is important that it is clearly stated what kind of affiliates the marketer is seeking, and what value it can deliver to the affiliate in terms of commission and content. With the right introduction to the right affiliates, a high percentage of the applicants are valuable to the marketer, and the marketer will spend less time declining useless ones.

Although the marketer's programme is made available on its website, many potential affiliates do not automatically apply to the programme. Therefore, the marketer must be proactive in the recruitment of affiliates. Particularly the larger media firms do not automatically apply to affiliate marketing programmes, so in order to recruit larger media as affiliates, the marketer must dedicate resources for contacting potential affiliates, maybe offering special content and commissions as incentives to join its programme. Moreover, it is important to both affiliates and marketers that the network actually has the best participants, and that the broker sets criteria for which affiliates and marketers can be part of the network.

In terms of exploiting the existing affiliate base, marketers must communicate to their affiliates on a regular basis. To facilitate a constant awareness and a close relationship to the affiliates, it is necessary to keep them up to date with the latest news about the products and services. Moreover, marketers must coordinate motivation initiatives for affiliates to continue actively promoting their services, very much in line with bonuses offered to a well-performing sales staff. Also efforts to synchronise with campaigns in other media demands planning. Affiliates must also have access to the relevant linking opportunities in terms of banners, text links, product links and even storefronts if applicable. Marketers should also 'educate' affiliates in the use of the links.

Having decided to use affiliate marketing, the marketer needs to plan the promotional mix, and each initiative must be coordinated with other elements of the marketing mix. In Figure 6.2, we have illustrated an illustrative outline for a one-year promotional strategy.

Affiliate marketing functions as an ongoing, underlying marketing tool, that should be synchronised with the other marketing and PR events that are more campaign-oriented and seasonal. In Figure 6.2, we have given examples of a few other marketing channels a marketer might use throughout the year. With an affiliate marketing programme, marketers have already established the relation to the affiliate, and they do not need to book the affiliate/media in advance. Additionally, every time marketers change creative material, introduce new products, or offer discounts, they only need to make the necessary changes centrally and the message will change instantly in the established affiliate marketing. And because of the tracking technology, marketers have an opportunity to measure the effect of each of the initiatives, and by this way optimise and re-evaluate their programme.

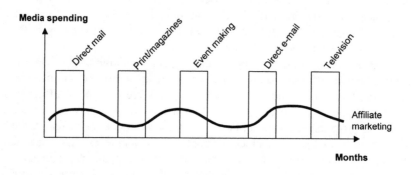

Figure 6.2   Promotional strategy with affiliate marketing

It is also important that marketers provide their affiliates with the best opportunity to place the links in the right context. Placement of the actual product occurs on the affiliate's website, for example through the link 'buy this book here', which can be presented as part of a book review. The affiliate in this situation has the 'shelf', and placement is decided by the affiliate, but often influenced by the marketer via the links it provides. This is comparable to traditional distribution that aims at recruiting the right resellers and placing the product in a tactically correct way in order to reach potential customers in their environment.

For the marketer, including the affiliate marketing programme in the marketing budget is not an uncomplicated measure. The fixed costs paid to the broker are easily calculated, but the commissions to the affiliates are directly variable to their performance and even if the underlying principle of performance-based payment is that marketing costs are variable (Forrester Research, 1999, 2001), marketers still need to control marketing costs and spending, particularly if the marketer does not know the actual quantifiable value of clicks or leads. Even sales can be difficult to quantify if the marketer cannot easily determine his own expenses for a sold product. There are two main ways of controlling the affiliate marketing spending: one is by regulating affiliate commissions in relation to affiliates' performance, and this way calculate a constant customer acquisition cost per affiliate segment, which is a variable cost. Another way is to set a maximum payout to affiliates, and when the budget is met the commission is set back to minimum, which can be considered a fixed cost in line with campaign expenses. The latter provides the marketer with full financial control by setting a fixed limit on affiliate marketing spending, but leaves little flexibility, and the marketer might lose affiliates that need to generate revenues on a continuous basis.

Many marketers have chosen to split the affiliate marketing budget in two: all fixed costs and costs for clicks are paid via the marketing budget, and all variable costs (leads and sales) are financed via the sales budget. This way, it is possible to control promotional costs, and still remain flexible towards affiliates.

Affiliate Marketing as a Lead Generator

By using affiliate marketing as a lead generator, it becomes a tool for the sales staff. Hence, marketers are able to actively follow up on information generated through their affiliate marketing programme. However, as this section explains, this is a more resource-demanding set-up and requires better IT systems (as well as the resources to follow up on leads).

When considering affiliate marketing as a lead generator, marketers should perceive their affiliates as representatives. This makes it important for them to share relevant information with their affiliates and provide them with advice regarding products and creative solutions that they can use in relation to their users, which should reflect positively on the marketer. In managing leads, and maintaining information on existing and potential customers, customer relation management (CRM) is often used (Andersen et al., 1999). The leads generated from a marketer's affiliate marketing programme should also go into this system. Hence, marketers typically generate leads from two sources – affiliate marketing as well as from their other resellers or own sales force. Both these sources should provide information for a marketer's CRM system. The relation between a marketer's affiliate management and CRM system is illustrated in Figure 6.3.

Andersen et al. (1999) divide a CRM system into three separate parts; the customer touch point, which in this case is the website, the application, which again is divided into the marketer's front office and back office, and finally data storing. In Figure 6.4, we present a simplified version of Andersen et al.'s (1999) CRM system in order to depict how marketers' tasks regarding affiliate marketing fit into the overall CRM system. Affiliate marketing can in principle be involved in all the tasks. In the previous section, we discussed the marketing aspects, and in this section we discuss the sales aspects. The back-office solution we discuss in the next section, where we view affiliate marketing as fully integrated in the firm.

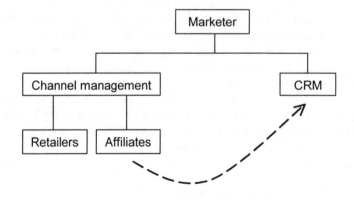

*Figure 6.3   Affiliate management in relation to customer relation
management*

Regarding the sales aspect, lead management is concerned with how the marketer redirect the leads delivered by affiliates to the right sales people, proposal generation is concerned with how the sales person use the leads and keeps the data stored in the CRM system, and (in)direct sales are concerned with the management of possible channel conflicts.

It can plausibly be argued that affiliates do not have an influence on the final sale, that it is important that marketers use resources to follow up on leads generated from affiliates. Therefore, when marketers use affiliate marketing, it is important to be able to make use of the information delivered. This requires that it be made clear to the affiliate what a good lead is, and that the right person has access to the data. Consequently, it is vital that the marketer's CRM system is properly integrated with the affiliate management system.

Where a marketer has integrated its lead functions with the call centre, so that every time a user registers a request for a purchase on its website, through an affiliate or directly, the call centre can rapidly follow up on the lead. Thus, proposal generation in the CRM system is the process where the marketer makes use of the lead to actually generate a sale. In the case of the call centre, the sales people take action on the lead and call the potential customer, and complete the deal. If the final purchase differentiates from the initial request, a new order sum is typed into the existing request, and the final confirmation must refer back to the affiliate that generated the lead, so it can receive the commission that corresponds to the amount of the final sale. By entering and confirming the final sale in the call centre, the marketer can keep track of which affiliates are generating the best leads/sales and reward them with higher commission rates, to ensure that they stay loyal.

Simultaneously, the marketer can focus its resources on sharing information and educating the best performing affiliates.

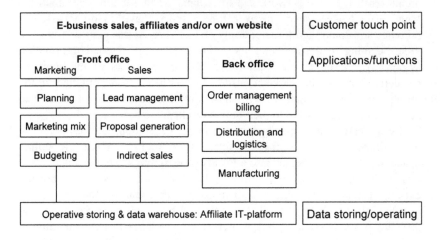

Source: Andersen et al., 1999

Figure 6.4   Affiliate marketing as part of a marketer's CRM system

The indirect sales model looks at marketers that make use of resellers to sell their products. This indirect model, in relation to affiliate marketing, can have a positive effect when it creates competition among the existing resellers and the affiliates trying to cover the demand in the market. However, if the resellers are essential to the marketer's business, as they often are, marketers must be able to minimise or prevent a negative reaction from resellers if they enter an affiliate marketing network.

The resellers could argue that affiliates take the profit margins they would have earned, and they would refuse to continue selling the marketer's products if it entered an affiliate marketing network. Marketers could be forced to decide against affiliate marketing due to a need to secure the existing distribution via offline shops that express strong discontent with an affiliate marketing solution. This discontent should in principle only be valid when affiliates take sales away from existing resellers and/or if it influences the resellers' profit margins. However, as the Internet grows, market share will for most companies shift partially to the Internet (Strauss and Frost, 1999), and if existing resellers wait a few more years before going online, they may find they cannot catch up with the marketer's online affiliates. Therefore, existing resellers often do have legitimate reason to be concerned about the marketer entering affiliate marketing.

A possible solution, to satisfy both existing resellers and the ambition of starting an affiliate marketing programme, would be to include the existing online resellers in the network and offer them a better commission than the 'new' affiliates. However, many offline resellers have no organised web presence and could therefore not easily be included. At this point in time, the orders coming to the marketer's website are through internal information systems passed on to the local shops that are members of the chain of resellers. That way the marketer ensures that its resellers are satisfied. In the fourth option we present, we will show how it is possible for marketers to secure a close relationship to their online resellers.

By integrating lead management, proposal generation, and resellers into the affiliate programme, the marketer has a tool for tying the online media/affiliates and resellers into a loyalty programme where the value of the relationship is high for both parties. When the marketer is online, but the existing resellers are not, and if they are essential to the marketer's distribution, the channel conflict is not only based on competition among different possible resellers, but also creates a challenge to implementing an affiliate marketing programme that can satisfy both online and offline resellers' needs.

Affiliate Marketing Fully Integrated

In this option, marketers integrate an affiliate marketing programme further with their processes, including order management billing, distribution and logistics, and manufacturing. When the marketer manages orders and billing to the end-user itself (without resellers), the actual contact with the customer is managed by the marketer itself, thus avoiding distribution of products to resellers. And as long as the affiliates never interfere with the physical distribution of products, distribution and manufacturing can be fully integrated with the marketer's CRM system. The affiliate marketing programme is not a source of channel conflict in this case, but is simply an extended sales function for the marketer.

Dell Computers is an example of a marketer using affiliate marketing in connection with the direct sales model (without resellers). Dell has divided its customers into two segments, SME customers and Large Accounts. The SME segment also includes private customers. The large accounts are handled by account managers, who set up a closed network between Dell and the client, so the client has an online consolidated statement for how much they have purchased, payments due, discounts etc., all in real time. Thus, Dell has no interest in including their strategic partners in the affiliate programme.

Therefore, Dell targets private customers and small/medium businesses in its affiliate marketing programme. This makes it important that Dell participates in active affiliate management and education. Dell manufactures only after orders are entered into the system, and in order for Dell to make use of CRM, it is a prerequisite that both Dell's front office and back office share the same data about customers, generated through affiliates.

When marketers decide for a full integration of affiliate marketing into the ERP systems, it is first and foremost a consideration concerning whether the information gathered via the affiliate is useful in each of the back-office processes. And in order to make the right fit to its existing set-up, the marketer must be aware of high initial investments in terms of education on all levels of the organisation. In the long run the consequences are related to managing the affiliate network, communicating and carrying out restriction policies, and not least being selective in which partners to invite into the network. With the optimal affiliate management, the marketer can decrease returned sales or useless leads, which are time consuming.

Reverse Affiliation

Contrary to the direct model, as described earlier, the indirect model contains opportunities for channel conflicts that need to be managed. Dell only has an online presence, and is therefore not dependent on long-term relationships with resellers. However, a large number of online marketers have a high path-dependency with regard to their distribution channels, also because the marketers have online as well as offline resellers.

In order to manage a possible channel conflict, TradeDoubler has been working with a 'reverse affiliate model'. This business model is not standardised, as reseller relations are unique in many aspects, for example billing and payments agreements, but in general it is possible to simplify a model, which can be applied in situations with similar channel conflicts. It is termed the 'reverse affiliate' model, illustrated in Figure 6.5.

The end-users goes to the marketer's website either directly or via the marketer's standard affiliate network. On the marketer's website it is possible to make the purchase, but in the case of reverse affiliation, it is, for example, made possible for the resellers to sell the products at a lower price than on the marketer's website, giving the end-user an incentive to go to the resellers. The marketer usually build a separate website where it is possible for the visitor to click on to one of the resellers. The marketer thus manages the channel conflict by redirecting end-users to online resellers, and the marketer becomes the 'affiliate', leading qualitative traffic to a third party (resellers). In the traditional affiliate network, the reseller is a possible affiliate, but now the reseller becomes the marketer, because the actual transaction is performed on the reseller's website. And the reseller must have implemented a tracking technology in order to validate the actual performance. In addition, resellers have access to an online statement similar to the traditional statistics a marketer has access to, and they can choose to integrate this information into their CRM systems as previously described.

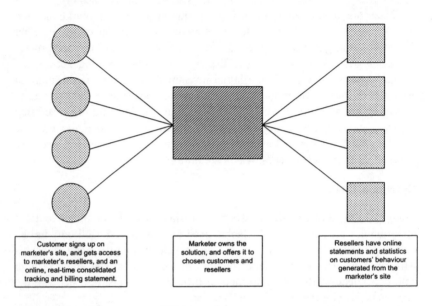

| Customer signs up on marketer's site, and gets access to marketer's resellers, and an online, real-time consolidated tracking and billing statement. | Marketer owns the solution, and offers it to chosen customers and resellers | Resellers have online statements and statistics on customers' behaviour generated from the marketer's site |

Figure 6.5   The reverse affiliate model

For this to be advantageous for the marketer, it must be able to control and add value to the network. It does so by owning and offering a brand-specific solution to both strategic partners/resellers and to chosen customers, so the affiliate supplier is undetectable in the network.

Consequently, the reverse affiliate network is structured as a one-to-many network, one affiliate and many marketers, as opposed to the standard affiliate network, where many affiliates link to many marketers (many-to-many), or many affiliates link to one marketer (many-to-one). In order for the marketer (who now acts as an affiliate) to keep control over the network they need to deliver an interesting marketplace with valuable buyers and suppliers that can acquire valuable information. If it is considered valuable enough the marketer could charge the resellers for being part of the network.

Resource Planning and Implementation

When a marketer has decided to actively use affiliate marketing to reach consumers or other interest groups, it must be implemented appropriately in the organisation in accordance with its purpose. Hence, if the ambition is only to use it as a marketing channel, the company does not need to involve other functions than the marketing department.

Generally, there are two ways to integrate affiliate marketing in the marketer's organisation. Either the marketing department allocates a number of people to focus on and have the entire responsibility for the affiliate marketing programme, or if the programme influences multiple functions in the organisation, the marketer must train several people in different functions and integrate the routines in existing processes. In general there are two modes of integration.

On one hand it can be decided that, for example, two dedicated people from the marketing department are to be responsible for affiliate partners in a given number of markets. They manage the daily affiliate marketing programme and recruit specific websites they are especially interested in, sometimes in collaboration with their media agency. The marketer only uses the programme as a marketing tool. This centralised administration makes it easy for the broker to communicate with the marketer. However, because of the superficial integration it is relatively easy to end the relationship for the marketer, with limited consequences.

On the other hand, a marketer can choose to integrate its affiliate marketing programme in the marketing function, the sales function, and, for example, the call centre, which could be outsourced to a third party. Just to set up the programme, TradeDoubler has completed a relatively deeper technical integration involving all functions, so everyone can access the necessary information. TradeDoubler has educated all three functions in the use of the programme, affirming a long-term commitment in the marketer's organisation. Not until the moment when the set-up is proved to be functioning technically and all involved employees are trained to use the programme, does the marketer start using it actively. Regardless of the level of integration, considering the competencies and know-how of the departments and people that are planned to become involved in the affiliate programme is also significant. The marketer must consider necessary training of staff and other involved parties like call centres, media agencies, web agencies, and other third-party providers.

6.3   CHAPTER CONCLUSION

When considering affiliate marketing, firms can adopt either a planned approach, where participation is considered and decided by top management, or an emergent approach, where participation is initiated lower in the organisation, on a small scale, and grows as it proves successful. However, due to start-up costs, especially for marketers, the planned approach is usually applied.

For affiliates, the main purpose of affiliate marketing is to generate revenues. It is estimated that by 2003, 83 per cent of online advertising will be at least partially performance-based. The main barrier affiliates face when considering affiliate marketing is that they fear their credibility will be compromised if they mix editorial content with commercial interests. The best solution may be to be honest with users about it, rather than attempt to cover it up. However, many affiliates, particularly professional media websites, are wary. For entertainment websites content integration may not be such a problem, but news websites have to be very careful about this. In these cases the best solution may be to only include commercial links on 'less intrusive' parts of the website.

Affiliates also need to accept that affiliate marketing brings with it some additional activities that require some resources. First of all, they need to keep the linking and implementation of banners in-house, since success in affiliate marketing requires a learning process of ongoing performance monitoring and content integration. Second, the performance-based payment structure requires a more elaborate budgeting and performance analysis process, because affiliates have more uncertainty with their revenues than with up-front impression-based payments.

Marketers considering affiliate marketing need to determine which interest groups they aim to reach, and what type of messages they want to send. If they have existing resellers, they need to consider how they will react, since affiliate marketing effectively involves bringing in 'new' resellers online. The best way to avoid this is to try and bring existing resellers in to the programme, or at least make sure they are not competing with affiliates for the same end-users under the same circumstances. Another major hindrance for some marketers is that they might have to give up some control of their brand when entering affiliate marketing. This brings the risk of the brand becoming diluted or that affiliates might have an incentive to misrepresent the brand. The best solution may simply be for marketers to accept that this involves a trade-off and that they need to give up some of this control in order to be successful. However, for some marketers allowing them the possibility of more tightly controlling the relationships may be a requirement, although tight management of hundreds or thousands of affiliate relationships can quickly become very resource-intense.

When a marketer decides on entering affiliate marketing, there are four basic set-up options to choose from. The first option involves simply using affiliate marketing as a marketing channel. This requires determining its place in the marketer's media mix. Affiliate marketing is mainly a tool for reaching niche audiences, and should run year-round to complement a marketer's seasonal campaigns. The second option involves affiliate marketing being used as a lead and sales generator, where affiliates generate leads for the marketer's sales staff to follow up on. This requires that affiliate marketing be integrated in the marketer's customer database or CRM system. The third option involves integrating affiliate marketing fully in the marketer's organisation, including billing, logistics and manufacturing, in order to ensure that sales generated are directly registered and managed by the marketer. The fourth option involves a marketer building an affiliate marketing model around its existing resellers. The marketer effectively functions as an affiliate by channelling potential customers to its resellers through its own website.

7. Explanation Model

In this chapter, we bring together the previous chapters in a holistic perspective and focus on the links among them. While Chapters 3 to 6 already do have some ties, we chose to present the problems from different angles, rather than building entirely on sequential input. Hence, we have not yet identified specific ties between the various roles, considerations and value elements firms can expect as part of an affiliate marketing network. Our basic assumption is that all four chapters are interrelated, meaning that the role a firm plays and how it fills out this role influences the value gained from affiliate marketing, for the firm as well as its partners. Similarly, the value a firm receives affects the considerations it makes in determining how to participate. We adopt the perspective of an affiliate and marketer respectively, and illustrate whether they gain value – positive or negative – from each of the value elements we identified in Chapter 4. We then indicate what types of roles affect these elements, and finally, how the value elements trigger strategic considerations. Table 7.1 illustrates this interrelation between value, roles and considerations for each of the two parties. The value elements are indicated as either positive or negative for each of the two parties, although needless to say this is something of a simplification. All roles are taken from our analysis in Chapter 3, all resources and underlying value elements taken from our analysis in Chapter 4, and all considerations from our analysis in Chapters 5 and 6. What is new are their interrelations.

Conclusively, we elaborate on the performance and objectives measures, which we presented in Figure 1.4. For each of the four measures: impression, click, lead, and sale, we illustrate different models of affiliate marketing that are useful when considering the four objectives and the desired performance. Building on these distinct models, we finish with an illustration of the effectiveness of affiliate marketing

7.1 VALUES, ROLES, AND CONSIDERATIONS

It should be noted that individual participants are only one of three units of analysis we apply in our research, meaning that not all value elements can be attributed to individual roles or considerations. Some value is generated at the level of the relationship or network, and cannot be properly explained at the individual level, hence there is not always a one-to-one relationship between roles, considerations and value elements. It should also be noted that Table 7.1 is a simplification, due to the complexity of the many elements and their links. Also, our research is mainly based on identifying value creation in the network. Thus, although we do have some negative value elements, these are typically only as a result of resource exchange where the other party receives a positive value. We have not looked specifically at identifying negative resources or underlying value elements. The consequences of this are that the value elements are predominantly positive. And finally, we have chosen to focus on marketers and affiliates, rather than the broker. Hence some of the value elements, particularly under brokerage and technology, are fulfilled by roles covered mainly by the broker. The figure is then further explained from the viewpoint of the affiliate and the marketer.

We cover affiliates and marketers respectively in the following sections. In focusing on the interrelations between value, roles and considerations, we do not cover the elements strictly in the order they appear in Table 7.1.

Affiliates

Affiliates' interests are aligned with marketers' through a performance-based payment structure that gives affiliates the opportunity to increase their commissions over time. This requires that they actively place links and monitor their own performance, changing the placement and types of links as they learn. The placing of these links is an important consideration for affiliates, since, in affiliate marketing, it is only on rare occasions outsourced to a third party and thus requires resources dedicated to implementation as well as ongoing monitoring and learning. This monitoring takes place through performance statistics, available to affiliates through the broker.

By trying out different links and testing the statistics, affiliates can, over time, improve their performance and thus commissions. However, the negative aspect of this payment structure for affiliates is that they bear the risk for the success of the marketer's advertising. This risk is a critical consideration for affiliates, since they need to determine how to budget with the revenue uncertainty, particularly large affiliates with expenses to cover. Affiliates do not get paid for creating branding for marketers, which effectively uses up a scarce resource of theirs – users' attention. However, affiliates have a role in deciding which links to place and where to place them. By choosing to use specific contextual links rather than general banners from marketers, they can minimise the unpaid branding they give away. At the same time, placing relevant contextual links is a key part of

Table 7.1 Values, roles and considerations

	Affiliate			Marketer		
	Value	Role	Consideration	Value	Role	Consideration
Brand						
Branding	-	Place links	Link format	+	Make links available	Type of affiliates
Brand association	+/-	Select marketer	Ethics/profile	+/-	Reject 'unethical' affiliates	Brand control
Performance-based payment						
Risk sharing	-	Integrate content to improve results	Budgeting	+	Develop commission structure	Determine set-up
Interest alignment	+	Place links and monitor performance	Increased activities	+/-	Communicate with affiliates	Allocation of resources
'Smart' network effects	+	Use data to improve results	Select best practice	+	Optimise on performance	Select best practice
Technology platform						
Marketing platform	+	Affiliate	Trust third party	+	Marketer	Trust third party
Connectivity	+	Place links		+	Implementation	
Scalability	+	Link to many		+	Be available	
Information						
End-user information	+	'Know' users	Sharing information	(+)	Collect information	Validity
Performance information	+	Monitor performance	Increased activities	+	Segment affiliates	Optimise

Brokerage

Brokerage	+	Receive payments		Trust third party	Pay for performance	Trust third party
Context-based sales						
Content integration	+	Place links	+	Increased activities	Develop 'creatives'	Match with affilliates
Ethics	-	Place links	+	Ethics/profile	Product placement	Profile
End-user relations						
Potential market	+	Attract users	+	Become reseller	Find resellers	Channel conflicts
Customer acquisition	+	Present marketers' offers	+	Select right offers	Make products available	Cost per click, lead and sale
'Ownership'	+	Build close user relationships	-	Fear of being bypassed	Follow-up on leads	Use of resources
Network relations						
Network access	+	Apply marketers	+/-	Long and short-term relations to marketers	Accept or reject affiliates	Resellers
Contractual flexibility	+/-	Ongoing placement of links	+/-	Opportunity cost	Segment affiliates	Affiliates' level of activity

affiliate marketing, and can significantly improve conversion rates, leading to higher commissions. A potential downside of these contextual links is that affiliates run the risk of losing credibility in the eyes of their users, who may not trust their content due to the integration of commercial interests. This is also an important consideration for affiliates. They must determine their profile and evaluate to what degree they can afford to integrate commercial interests and content. Some affiliates may have to keep this integration to certain 'non-intrusive' parts of their website. It is also important to be up-front with users about any commercial interests.

It can be valuable for affiliates to form partnerships with marketers with strong brands, because it can boost their own credibility in the eyes of users to be associated with them. However, selecting a marketer with a questionable brand can actually harm an affiliate's credibility. This requires that affiliates invest time in their role of selecting marketers to partner with, which ideally should match their ethical profile as well as user base. It is valuable to affiliates that they have a number of different marketers to choose from, all in one place. This also makes it simple to shift marketers if they are unhappy with the partnership, without any prior warning. Although marketers can do the same, affiliates prefer this contractual flexibility to a tighter control.

Selecting a marketer makes it important that affiliates 'know' their users, also in order to use this information to improve performance. An important role of affiliates is to attract users, through their content and own marketing efforts, since they are the foundation for generating commissions. The standardisation of the affiliate marketing platform and connectivity of the Internet makes this simple and efficient, although it can be difficult to attract users due to the 'information overload' of the Internet. Once these users have been attracted, affiliates should seek to build close relationships with them, perhaps through a community-type expertise and focus. This should allow affiliates to increase customer acquisition rates, and equally important to hold on to the 'ownership' of these customers, so that they become a source of continuous revenues, rather than one-time customers.

Marketers

For marketers, one of the most valuable aspects of affiliate marketing is that they transfer much of their advertising risk to affiliates. This requires that they can quantify the value of leads and sales in order to develop a commission structure that gives them the margins and/or customer acquisition costs they want. This should be preceded by an important consideration by marketers in determining what their objectives are and thus which type of set-up they should adopt.

A critical consideration for a marketer with existing resellers is how they will perceive its participation in affiliate marketing. If they are strongly against it, marketers may decide to choose a reverse affiliation set-up, which is built around existing resellers, rather than recruiting new ones.

Affiliate marketing appears to provide relatively low customer acquisition costs, which is valuable, especially given the high costs of online customer acquisition costs through other methods. However, it is important that marketers maintain a website that maintains users' interests and makes it easy for them to find what they came for. Once customers have been acquired or leads have been generated, marketers must follow them up, in order to secure long-term customers. It can be a problem for marketers that affiliates continue to 'own' customers, thus having to pay them commission on all future sales. This is also something that must be taken into consideration when designing a commission structure.

While it is valuable to marketers that an affiliate marketing network gives them access to thousands of potential affiliates, it is important that they invest the resources in rejecting affiliates that they perceive as unethical or that may dilute their brand. Affiliates with a strong credibility among their users, on the other hand, can significantly improve a marketer's performance. Once approving affiliates, marketers should actively segment them according to their relative performance, since affiliate commissions can be changed instantly if necessary. The performance information on affiliates is valuable to marketers in this regard, but marketers need to allocate resources to monitoring this information. It is a benefit to marketers that the broker takes care of this function, but their fees obviously cut into margins and require some volume in the programme to pay off.

Marketers receive free branding from affiliates through the awareness among users their links and images create, which is not explicitly paid for. However, they typically have to pay the large affiliates higher click payments in order to partially compensate them for this. Affiliates do accept giving marketers some branding, because promoting a marketer along with the products they are selling or the memberships they are offering often results in a higher performance. To maximise this effect, marketers should develop creative materials – product images, storefronts, banners and text – that reflect the value to users of what they offer. They should give affiliates a wide selection of these creatives/messages, so that they can choose the ones that fit their audience the best.

7.2 AFFILIATE MARKETING MODELS

Figure 1.4 illustrated the performances and objectives in affiliate marketing. The marketer active in affiliate marketing holds some objectives, which we have broken into four prioritised levels: exposure, recognition, attitude, and exchange. Performance is considered by the responses of the end-user, which we also broke into four prioritised levels: attention, interest, desire, and action. Both objectives and performance were compared in a matrix, so that different objectives have corresponding performances. The correspondence between objectives and performance are measured by four variables: impression, click, lead, and sale.

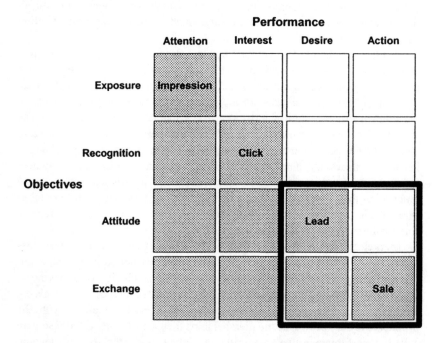

Figure 7.1   Objectives and performance in affiliate marketing

It should be noted that the primary focus areas of affiliate marketing are lead and sales-generating activities, see Figure 7.1, which should also be a marketer's key reasons to become active in affiliate marketing. However, once the marketer is active it should take advantage of consolidating all its online activities into one administration tool, and differentiate the conditions for payments, creatives etc. for each objective. To illustrate this we have extended Figure 4.2 on how to make a performance-based segmentation of affiliates to also include objective-based segmentation of affiliates.

Table 7.2   *Objective and performance-based segmentation of affiliates*

		CPM (€)	Click (€)	Lead (€)	Sale (%)	Max CPA (€)
	Gold (3%+)		0.2	1	10	30
Public programme	Silver (1–3%)		0.1	2	10	30
	Bronze (0–1%)		0.0	2	10	30
	Large	0.05	0.3			
Campaign programme	Medium	0.03	0.2			
	Small	0.0	0.2			
	SME clients			1	15	40
Strategic programme	Resellers			1	15	40
	Government			1	15	40

Each programme level indicates the objective of the activities, where in Table 7.2 the public programme is focused on generating interest, desire, and action; thus, the affiliates are rewarded for click, lead, and sale. In addition, each affiliate is placed in a sub-segment according to the conversion rate from interest to action, in order to optimise and control spending so a cost per action (CPA) never exceeds the maximum acceptable amount. The campaign programme is focused on creating attention and interest, thus affiliates in this segment are rewarded for cost per thousand impressions (CPM) and click. However, it is still critical to optimise spending and the choice of different segments to remain the opportunity for negotiation. Finally, the strategic programme is focused on generating desire and action via established relationships that need to be handled separately, and under different criteria. This could be an integrated link from a client's extranet, to make the ordering process easier and at the same time offer a discount or a return commission, administered by the broker. Alternatively, it could be an existing reseller that needs to be treated favourably in order to avoid channel conflicts.

   In the following we illustrate four affiliate marketing models: exposure-, recognition-, attitude-, and exchange-based affiliate marketing, and for each of four different objectives we compare with the corresponding performances. All four objectives have overlapping performances, and because it is possible to reward the same affiliate for all four: impression, click, lead, and sale, a recognition-based affiliate model could easily generate action (sales). Nevertheless, for explanatory reasons we explain each of the models separately.

Exposure-based Affiliate Marketing

Exposure-based affiliate marketing is the simplest form of the genre, and is very similar to traditional banner advertising, as exposure is achieved simply by being visible with a graphical element in online media that are selected based on demographic segmentation principles. Because affiliate marketing technologies make it possible to track click, lead, and sale, the marketer can evaluate the media on multiple measures to better evaluate, negotiate, and recruit the best performing affiliates/media for future campaign activities.

Together with the media agency or the affiliate broker, the marketer typically selects media that can reach as many people as possible in the preferred demographic segment. This typically demands a good number of hours of planning and negotiating in order to implement the campaign, thus an exposure-based affiliate marketing network consists of a relatively smaller number of affiliates that are active in a short period of time.

Figure 7.2   Exposure-based affiliate marketing model

Attention is simply achieved each time a visitor is exposed to the marketer's banner on one of the campaign affiliates. Such a model is simply a website with a top-banner, as illustrated in Figure 7.2.

Recognition-based Affiliate Marketing

Recognition-based affiliate marketing is also a relatively simple form of affiliate marketing. The recognition is measured when a user shows interest by clicking on the link to the marketer, and the marketer rewards the affiliates every time they bring a visitor to their web page. The affiliates generally achieve the best results when they integrate the link into the web page's existing content, for example, a subcategory that is suitable for the marketer's message and thus in correlation with the visitor's interest. The link is not dependent on a specific banner format, and the visitor can click into the marketer's site via, for example, a text link in an article. Figure 7.3 illustrates a simple click-through from an affiliate web page, with a content of mobile services to a related page on a leading telecom provider's different web pages.

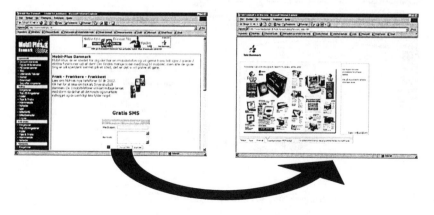

Figure 7.3   Recognition-based affiliate marketing model

Thus, recognition is typically measured by click-through rates. In addition, marketers find it interesting to measure how deeply the visitor goes into its website before actually performing a lead, and this evaluates the level of recognition delivered from different affiliates. This is simply measured by placing checkpoints on selected pages, which quantifies when the visitor comes to the selected page.

Attitude-based Affiliate Marketing

Attitude-based affiliate marketing is the next level of integration between the affiliate and the marketer. The attitude is measured when the end-user performs a lead that shows a desire for the marketer's product or services. When focusing on generation of leads, the marketer must make things easy and relevant for the end-user. This is most generally achievable in two ways: when the marketer's link is made available on an affiliate site with a closely-related content, and/or when the affiliate has integrated the link or functionality, leading to the generation of the lead, on its website.

In Figure 7.4, an end-user visits a vertical affiliate site, www.denford.net, with a specific content of financial loans, and on this site, the end-user is recommended to visit the marketer, www.etrade.dk, where the visitor performs a lead by applying for an account with E*trade.

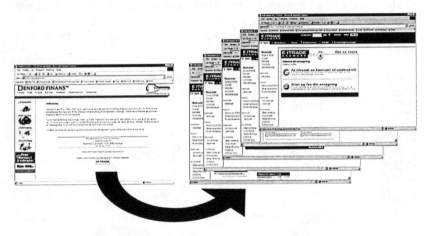

Figure 7.4   Attitude-based vertical affiliate model

In this case, the end-user is directed to the merchant's front page, and in order to perform the lead the end-user must go through a number of steps on the marketer's website, before the lead is completed. Regularly, the marketers' experience is that the visitors never complete the leads. Too often this is due to the fact that the visitor is taken away from his/her initially preferred affiliate site and situated in a new location, where there is no apparent connection to the interest discovered on the affiliate's site, and the desire, for the end-user, to complete an application seems irrelevant and out of context.

Therefore, affiliates and marketers have more success with generating leads when graphical elements and functionalities are closely integrated, and the visitor is performing most of the application (lead) on the affiliate's site in the same context as initially chosen, and not until the final confirmation is the user directed to the merchant's site, where he or she immediately can complete the application.

The example in Figure 7.5 illustrates how an affiliate has integrated the merchant's link in a categorised text link (health insurances), and the visitor is directed into a sub-segment where he or she can finalise the lead in the specific sub-category.

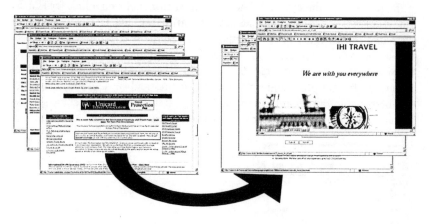

Figure 7.5   Attitude-based integrated affiliate marketing model

Nevertheless, the end-user is still taken away from his or her initial choice of website. This is not necessarily incorrect, but in order to build sustainable affiliate relations, the marketers must be aware that many end-users have strong preferences to specific affiliate sites that they visit on a daily basis. In such cases, the relationship will be much more beneficial for all parties, if the visitor can perform the action (lead or sale) preferred by the marketer, on the affiliate site. This is achievable in the exchange-based affiliate marketing model.

Exchange-based Affiliate Marketing

Exchange-based affiliate marketing is the most integrated form of affiliate marketing as the visitor never leaves the affiliate site, but performs the transaction via a micro-site, which is fully integrated into the affiliate site. The exchange is measured when the visitor completes a sales action in the micro-site, and an exchange has occurred between the marketer and the end-user. When building this micro-site, the marketer and the affiliate can choose to have the micro site pop up when the end-user clicks on the link or they can construct the micro-site to be presented as a sub-category on the affiliate site, as is the case in Figure 7.6.

In case of a micro-site that pops up, it is convenient for the visitor because he or she is not taken away from the affiliate site and the two sites are separate from each other. In this way, the end-user can easily return to the affiliate site, when he or she has performed the action in the micro-site. Alternatively, the micro-site is presented in a separate sub-category on the affiliate's site. In the case in Figure 7.6, the visitor clicks on a link for Haburi (the marketer) on www.netposten.dk (the affiliate), and is led to a Haburi shop in a sub-category of www.netposten.dk. Here the end-user can complete an order with Haburi, and never feels that he or she is leaving www.netposten.dk. However, the action of the end-user is transferred to Haburi's affiliate programme via the micro-site, and in addition, the order and personal information from the end-user is transferred into Haburi's CRM system, even though the visitor never visited Haburi's website.

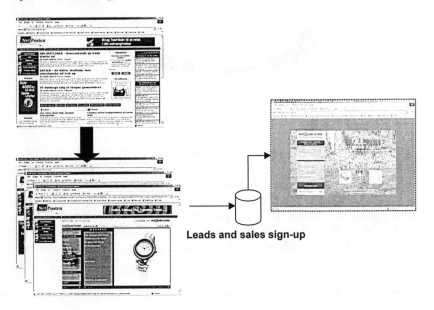

Leads and sales sign-up

Figure 7.6   Exchange-based affiliate marketing model

In such set-ups, affiliates act as distributors of the marketer's goods and services. In order to evaluate the success of an exchange-based affiliate marketing model, the marketer should, thus, not only consider conversion rates from clicks to sales, but, on a continuous basis, put higher emphasis on evaluating whether the network of affiliates/distributors lives up to the online distribution strategy, and secure the distribution network in the long term. These considerations can be compared to traditional retail strategies where, for example, fast-moving consumer goods companies are competing on the best distribution channels.

7.3 EFFECTS OF AFFILIATE MARKETING

We conclude this chapter by summarising the effects of each of the affiliate marketing models. We illustrate how the effects of affiliate marketing out-perform traditional marketing in terms of attention, interest, desire and action, if competently managed.

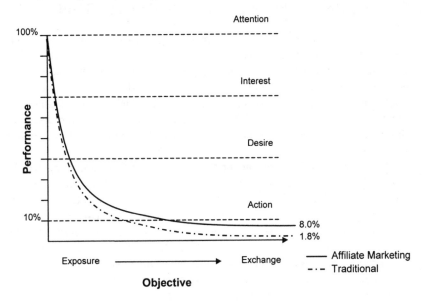

Figure 7.7   Effects of affiliate marketing

In Figure 7.7, we illustrate how each level of affiliate marketing improves the results, and if applied appropriately, each affiliate marketing model contributes with a positive effect on the conversion rates from impressions to clicks, to leads, to sales. As an effect, the conversion rate from attention to action increases considerably in comparison to traditional online marketing. And as a consequence, the marketer will experience a significant increase in the return on its marketing investment. In Figure 7.7 we have illustrated this by an increase in actions from 1.8 per cent to 8.0 per cent. Of course, not all improvements are this evident, some are more and some are less. These conversion rates will vary from case to case, but the intentions behind affiliate marketing will remain the same, to build profitable and long-term relations between marketers and affiliates.

As explained throughout the book, there are many value elements and many factors that influence the success of participating in an affiliate marketing network. Accordingly, with an understanding of the dynamics presented in this book, potential participants, marketers and/or affiliates, should be well capable of planning how and whether to participate and how to exploit the opportunities that exist and arise with affiliate marketing.

7.4   TAKING AFFILIATIONS ONE STEP FURTHER

One of the great benefits of affiliate marketing is clearly that the marketers and affiliates can instantaneously measure the effects of their online activities. Also, it will always remain a priority for the marketers to validate and optimise their marketing spending. Anchored in a basic need for marketers and media to continuously improving their online business, it seems very likely that many of the principles of affiliate marketing discussed throughout this book will also be evident throughout multiple online activities.

The essential value element for the future of affiliate marketing will be the tracking technology that makes it possible to measure all consumer behaviour and thus performance. Hence, many aspects of affiliate marketing will merge into a number of other online activities, such as short-term campaigns, sponsorships, strategic partnerships, etc., and the resemblance for all activities will be the fact that all performances are measured and evaluated, regardless of the objectives and the payment structure.

Based on our discussion about objectives and performances, and the strategic considerations of the marketer and the affiliate, we will, in the following, look into how in the future affiliate marketing will blend into multiple online business models, and how it will affect both affiliates and marketers.

Objectives and Performances

Earlier in this chapter we outlined four affiliate marketing models: exposure-based, recognition-based, attitude-based, and exchange-based. These models originated from the matrix presented in Figure 7.1. Both objectives and performance were compared in the matrix, and different objectives have corresponding performances.

The attitude-, and exchange-based models were argued to be the two primary affiliate marketing models. However, with the advanced tracking technology emerging into, for example, short-term campaign activities, the objectives of an exposure-based affiliate model will have multiple performances, not 'only' attention (measured by the number of impressions), but also interest (click), desire (leads), and action (sale) will be measures of performance. Consequently, each affiliate, each graphical element, each placement of the ad, etc. will be measured up against its ability to generate leads and sales for the marketer, regardless of the payment structure. And the information will instantaneously be accessible to both the marketer and the media.

This does not mean that sponsorships, campaigns, etc. will be paid in accordance to generated leads and sales. However, the interesting exercise for the marketer and the media will be to establish a parallel understanding for the objectives of the different online activities, so the payment structure, the message, and the creative material correspond. Typically this is planned and administrated by the media agencies. Nevertheless, when the performance measures are instantly available due to the tracking technology, it allows for the best performing solutions, even in a so-called short-term campaign, to remain active as long as good results are shown. Hence, the planning of online campaigns will become more flexible, and the marketers' marketing and sales activities will form as an emergent process, corresponding with the knowledge attained in the active campaign.

Consequently it could be argued that for this to work in the long run, marketers and media could just as well form a partnership where the payment structure is based on leads and sales, which also occur in relationships that have found their equilibrium. However, most media will continuously be organised to control and sell ad space, if not by internal sales staff then via mediators (media agencies, affiliate brokers, banner networks, etc.). In doing so, the media will constantly seek to optimise and improve their online business.

Before we go further into how the emergence of improved tracking technologies will affect affiliates and marketers respectively, we briefly emphasise that different equilibria will occur between the two parties.

Because each marketer and each affiliate is unique in its business models, objectives, profit margins, organisational structure, etc. it would be very incorrect to consider a general equilibrium that can explain how the different players should optimise their online businesses in terms of payment structure, network characteristics, communications, graphical elements and functionalities. A high complexity between multiple parties doesn't allow for one common solution, instead, we will most likely experience many different equilibria based on industries and objectives. Consequently, the matrix presented in Figure 7.1 will not be as stable as first suggested. Exposure-based models can easily be paid per click as opposed to per impression and attitude (lead-generating) campaigns can be paid per impression, which is illustrated in Figure 7.8.

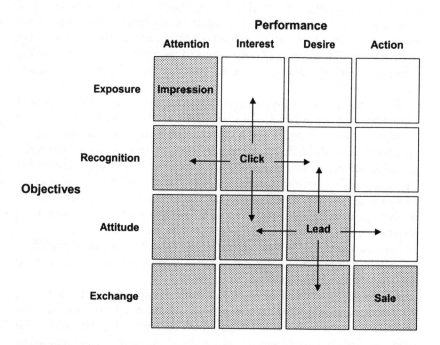

Figure 7.8   Dynamics in the objectives–performance matrix

The payment structure is of course subject to the bargaining power between the two parties, but when the tracking technology validates the performance for both parties it will automatically set the grounds for a sustainable relationship, and it will be evident for both parties what payments and conversion rates create an equilibrium. With this in focus, we examine the future of affiliate marketing from affiliates, and marketers, perspectives in turn, starting with the affiliates.

Affiliates

Most affiliate networks are organised so one marketer has many affiliates, and the marketer can thus start optimising and decide which affiliates are the most valuable to work with. For the largest affiliates that make their primary income on campaigns, the organisation is the reverse; each affiliate recruits many marketers to fill a maximum inventory (ad space). Therefore it is important to the affiliate to have a stronger saying in the selection process. Thus the largest affiliates will seek to own the tracking technology in order to deliver the statistics/results of a campaign, and in order to be able to argue why their communication channel is appropriate for the marketer. With the technology on hand, the affiliate will get the opportunity to advise the marketer, based on the effectiveness of the campaign with regards to graphical elements, placements, communication, and maybe most important revenues generated from leads and sales. Hence, the affiliate will be able to go into a strategic dialogue with the marketer, which has previously been done by the media agency, on behalf of the different communications media.

To justify the idea that communications media will focus more enthusiastically on affiliate marketing and start investing in the technology, we briefly present three of the media's potential benefits. Each benefit below can be considered individually; however, maybe the largest benefit per se is the fact all the benefits are combined and supporting each other.

Reduce spare inventory with the ability to offer attractive hybrid deals to advertisers

The communications media can start offering advertisers deals based on combined measures of CPM, CPC and CPA, and this way optimise a potential spare inventory.

Strong tool to administer all online relationships

All relationships such as sponsorships, campaigns, integrated content partnerships, e-mail marketing, etc. can be measured thus helping select which relationships are most beneficial, both for the advertiser and the media. Maybe some advertisers are not performing in a certain medium at a certain time, and the communications media would be able to focus on the better performers, or alternatively suggest new ways of working together. The best-performing relationships perceptibly develop into long-term partnerships, and it is easier to sell to the same marketer twice, rather than recruiting a new one. Hence, the communications media can evaluate the value they bring their advertisers, thereby increasing their own revenues accordingly.

Recognised third-party validation

By having a third party to set the standards and deliver data provides a parallel criterion for measurements, which both parties can trust. This will in most cases free up costs and resources for both parties and form stable relationships.

Marketers

As already proposed, the use of affiliate marketing will flourish into many different online activities, and different affiliate marketing models will be created, characterised by different industries and different objectives. Whether the activity is a short-term campaign, a sponsorship, or strategic partnership, the marketer will focus on optimising its spending, and thus seek to perform sustainable marketing and sales activities.

Let us assume that a computer hardware company is marketing and selling its products on the Internet and, in order to be profitable, the maximum cost per order the profit margins allow is 5 per cent. However, it is not possible for the company to advertise in the preferred media on a sales commission, but they must pay per click. The hardware company's average order sum is €2,500, and the click payment to the media is €0.3. Table 7.2 below presents the equilibrium conversion rate from click to sales, assuming a fixed cost per click.

Table 7.3   Conversion rates and costs

Conversion rates from click to sale (sales rate) (%)	Cost of clicks for one generated sale (€ 0,3 per click*100/sales rate) (€)	Maximum cost per order (€ 2500*5%) (€)
0.1	300	125
0.2	150	125
0.24	125	125
0.3	100	125

In the above example, the computer hardware company can only afford to continuously advertise in the media that has a minimum conversion rate of 0.24 per cent, otherwise they will have to pay less per click or alternatively a sales commission. Of course not all media will perform to the acceptable conversion rate and the marketer will thus start focusing its resources on the best performing media. As long as the media delivers an acceptable conversion rate that fulfils the equilibrium, the payment structure (pay per click or pay per sale) doesn't matter, the two parties could in principle agree on an impression-based payment as long as the cost per order does not exceed €125.

However, if the marketer was producing fast-moving consumer goods, and its primary distribution channel was offline, then the company's objective would typically be to generate leads. In such a case they would just calculate a maximum cost per lead, and the relationship to the media would be successful as long as the final cost per lead doesn't exceed an estimated lead value.

The conversion rates to leads are typically higher than to sales, the value of the lead varies with industries and objectives, and the marketers' ability to convert a lead into a sale varies. All these factors are essential for the marketer's success. Hence, numerous variations affect the ideal equilibrium between the marketer and the affiliate, and the value per click will differentiate from case to case. Hence, in order to build sustainable relationships between marketers and affiliates, the payment structures require flexibility.

7.5 THE FUTURE OF AFFILIATE MARKETING

In this final section, we will evaluate affiliate marketing in a wider perspective, and reflect on how it may develop in the future. As we have concluded earlier, the phenomenon offers value to participants in certain areas, and may thus live up to the predictions by research firms of strong further growth over the next few years, although more research is still needed in this area. However, affiliate marketing is currently purely a World Wide Web phenomenon, making its scope fairly limited. According to Jupiter Communications (2000a), online advertising only makes up about 3 per cent of the total advertising market (in the USA), while TV makes up about 35 per cent. What is interesting about affiliate marketing, though, is that the problems it seeks to solve are not limited to the Web, but are generally applicable to all large commercial media, including TV. These problems, as mentioned in our introduction, concern an overload of (irrelevant) marketing messages to consumers as well as a lack of marketing accountability. Based on marketers' needs to reach their target audiences, tremendous amounts are being spent on marketing through a variety of media (Jupiter Communications, 2000a), but accountability is often lacking (Zyman, 1999). The question is whether affiliate marketing, or a related phenomenon, could alleviate some of these problems.

Affiliate marketing addresses the aforementioned problems through performance-based payment, where the media are paid mainly for sales or leads, rather than impressions. The reason why affiliate marketing was invented for the Web is that a technology that allows extensive tracking of transactions across several parties is a prerequisite. This tracking is what makes accountability possible. Hence, affiliate marketing is in principle only possible in digitalised networks, where this kind of tracking is feasible. On a large scale, the Internet is such a network. Over the past seven years, commercial use of the Internet has been conducted almost exclusively through the Web, although e-mail has also played a smaller commercial role. However, both are effectively limited to the use of a PC by end-users. In the near future, by all accounts, there will be a surge in other Internet-driven media. Software platforms have already been developed for mobile phones ('3G') and TVs (ITV), and are facing rapid commercialisation in the near future. With these devices all connected to the Internet, all interactions between individual devices can be tracked. This would in principle make it possible for affiliate marketing to be conducted in these media. However, we believe that the following characteristics are also necessary for an Internet-based medium in order to allow the use of affiliate marketing:

- Commercial viability
- Interactivity between marketer and end-user
- Decentralisation
- User-friendly interface.

First and foremost, marketers must be able to use the medium commercially. This is not always possible, due to regulation or other factors. Interactivity is necessary as the end-user must be able to react to stimuli and perform a traceable action on the marketer's market space using the media. In order to allow for 'performance', affiliates must have some degree of autonomy in their decision-making, which requires at least partial decentralisation in the contextual network. And finally, while not critical, a user-friendly interface will presumably play a significant role in the scope of possibilities affiliate marketing can bring to the media.

So do any media besides the Web fulfil these criteria? We think the two aforementioned emerging media – ITV and 3G mobile phones/devices – are possible candidates. ITV is an advancement of an existing marketing channel. Marketers have traditionally used TV as a push media for mass marketing, but with ITV's opportunities for interactions with end-users, marketers can also start using 'pull technology' marketing methods, where users themselves take action according to their interests. On the other hand, mobile phones are not yet really established as a commercial medium and are emerging from an existing pull-type technology. However, the new 3G mobile phones and devices can be viewed as an increasingly commercialised medium due to an increasing quantity of functions, including communication (phone calls, e-mails, etc.), shopping and order delivery.

Table 7.3   *Emerging digitalised media's adoption of affiliate marketing*

Necessary Characteristics	ITV	3G Phones and Other Mobile Devices
Commercial	TV is accepted and used as a commercial media, with new possibilities for interactive transactions, affiliate marketing is a feasible opportunity.	Until now, mobile devices have only to a very limited degree functioned as a commercial marketing medium, so the question is how marketers will make use of this medium in their media mix.
Interactivity	ITV is interactive (by definition), and will presumably merge some PC and Internet functionalities, making affiliate marketing feasible. There is an increasing opportunity for marketers to exercise pull-technology-based marketing via the TV, by allowing users to become the initiative takers. However, the ITV will presumably continue to be used for mass marketing. Thus, the challenge is to a high degree conceptual, at least at first.	The interactions are evident with 3G devices, but the character of the actual hardware effectively limits the interaction potential early on. Mobile technology has been built on pull-type technology from its beginning, and it is for this reason possible for end-users to initiate action and perform a traceable action on the marketer's market space using the medium.
Decentralisation	Due to controlled distribution channels, TV has a history of oligopoly. Hence, ITV is very far from the Web's ultra decentralised structure where practically anyone can deliver content.	As in the case with TV, mobile technology is controlled by few players, setting limits on the number and types of affiliates likely to emerge.
User-friendly Interface	The highly developed TV screens and remote control technologies facilitate a very user-friendly interface, maybe more user-friendly than the PC.	Because of the handiness of mobile devices there are limited user-friendly interfaces. They are highly convenient, though, because users can carry them around.

In both cases the question is the same: will these media be able to adapt to affiliate marketing as they in turn build on technology that makes it feasible? However, there are significant differences in the two media that must be taken into consideration when determining the future adoption of affiliate marketing in each of them. Building on the necessary characteristics described above for affiliate marketing to be successful, Table 7.3 presents an evaluation of the compatibility of the existing notion of affiliate marketing to the two media: ITV and 3G mobile devices.

The two media both seem to some degree to fulfil the basic characteristics that we think are necessary for adopting affiliate marketing, so this may become a very real possibility in the future. The figure illustrates that the highest obstacle may be the relative lack of decentralised control in both media. One of the reasons why affiliate marketing works well on the Web is that it is extremely cheap to publish content, so anyone with a free homepage in a community or portal can become an affiliate. This leads to a combination of niche affiliates and scalability that is unique for the Web. With both ITV and 3G mobile phones/devices, there is much more centralisation. Presumably, there will not be the millions of affiliates we see on the Web. There are battles going on as to who will provide content for these media, but a number of large firms will probably share this role, allowing them to become affiliates and sell marketers' products. However, due to their size they may not be willing to accept a pure performance-based payment structure, and will probably have the bargaining power with marketers to set many of the terms. Thus the relationships may have more the appearance of a co-branded marketing partnership than the type of affiliate marketing relationship described in this book.

References

Aaker, D.A. (1991), *Managing Brand Equity*, New York, NY: The Free Press.

Alexander, E.R. (1995), *How Organizations Act Together*, Luxembourg: Gordon and Breach Publishers.

Al-Kibsi, G., de Boer, K., Mourshed, M., and Rea, N.P. (2001), 'Putting Citizens On-line, Not in Line', *McKinsey Quarterly*, (2), 64–73.

Andersen, A., Andreasen, M.D., and Jacobsen, P.Ø. (1999), *The CRM Handbook: From Group to Multi-individual*, Copenhagen, Denmark: PriceWaterhouseCoopers..

Argyris, C. and Schön, D.A. (1978), *Organizational Learning: A Theory of Action Perspective*, Reading, MA: Addison-Wesley.

Armstrong, A. and Hagel III, J. (1996), 'The Real Value of Online Communities', *Harvard Business Review*, **74** (3), 134–140.

Azeez, W. (2001), 'Cheap and Cheerful', *Guardian*, 18 January.

Baker, W.L., Lin, E., Marn, M.V., and Zawada, C.C. (2001), 'Getting Prices Right on the Web', *McKinsey Quarterly*, (2), 54–63.

Barsh, J., Kramer, E.E., Maue, D., and Zuckerman, N. (2001), 'Magazine's Home Companion', *McKinsey Quarterly*, (2), 82–91.

Belch, G.E. and Belch, M.A. (1995), *Advertising and Promotion – An Integrated Marketing Communications Perspective*, 3rd edn, Chicago, IL: Irwin.

Bennet, R.E. (2001), 'How the Internet Will Help Large-Scale Assessment Reinvent Itself', *Education Policy Analysis Archives*, **9** (5).

Boston Consulting Group (BCG) (2000a), *Online Retailing in the Nordic Countries: Seizing the Internet Advantage*, Market report, January.

Boston Consulting Group (BCG) (2000b), *The Race for Online Riches: E-Retailing in Europe*, Market report, February.

Brown, S. (1995), *Postmodern Marketing*, London, UK: International Thomson Business Press.

Bruner, R.E., Harden, L. and Heyman, B. (2001), *NetResults.2 – Best Practices for Web Marketing*, Indianapolis, IN: New Riders Publishing.

Bucklin, C.B., DeFalco, S.P., DeVincentis, J.R. and Lewis III, J.P. (1996), 'Are You Tough Enough to Manage Your Channels?', *McKinsey Quarterly*, (1), 104–114.

Burt, R.S. (1992), 'The Social Structure of Competition', in Nohria, N. and Eccles, R.G. (eds), *Networks and Organizations: Structure, Form and Action*, Boston, MA: Harvard Business School Press.

Cartellieri, C., Parsons, A.J., Rao, V., and Zeisser, M.P. (1997), 'The Real Impact of Internet Advertising', *McKinsey Quarterly*, (3), 44–52.

Choo, C.W. (1998), *The Knowing Organization*, New York, NY: Oxford University Press.

Colley, R.H. (1961), *Defining Advertising Goals for Measured Advertising Results*, New York, NY: Association of National Advertisers.

Corey, E.R. (1992), *Marketing Strategy – An Overview*, Case Study No. 9-579-054, Boston, MA: Harvard Business School Publishing.

Cotlier, M. (2001), 'Making Affiliate Online Marketing Programmes Work', *Catalog Age*, 1 January.

Coupey, E. (2001), *Marketing and the Internet – Conceptual Foundations*, Upper Saddle River, NJ: Prentice Hall.

Cross, K. (1999), 'Whither the Banner', *Business 2.0*, December.

Donaton, S. (2000), 'Ad Deals that Blur Content Line are No Substitute for Creativity', *Advertising Age*, **71** (49), 32.

Ebenkamp, B. (2001), 'Return to Peyton Placement', *Brandweek*, **42** (23), 10–17.

Engel, J.F., Blackwell, R.D., and Miniard, P.W. (1993), *Consumer Behavior*, 7th edn, Fort Worth, TX: Dryden Press.

Evans, P.B. and Wurster, T.S. (1997), 'Strategy and the New Economics of Information', *Harvard Business Review*, **75** (5), 71–83.

Findahl, O. (2001), *Swedes and the Internet – Year 2000*, Research Report, Gävle, Sweden: World Internet Institute.

FitzRoy, P.T. (1976), *Analythical Methods for Marketing Management*, London, UK: McGraw-Hill.

Ford, D., Gadde, L.E., Håkansson, H., Lundgren, A., Snehota, I., Turnbull, P., and Wilson, D. (1998), *Managing Business Relationships*, Chichester, UK: John Wiley & Sons.

Forrester Research (1999), *New Affiliate Marketing Models*, Research Report, October, Cambridge, MA.

Forrester Research (2001). *Online Advertising Eclipsed*, Research Report, January, Cambridge, MA.

Gehman, J. (2001a), 'Affiliate Marketing Meets the Channel', *ClickZ Network (www.clickz.com)*, 2 March.

Gehman, J. (2001b), 'Market-Share Update: Affiliate Marketing on the Move', *ClickZ Network (www.clickz.com)*, 16 March.

Gren, F., Maor, D., and Ubinas, L.A. (2001), 'Late Edition: Another Chance for Newspapers on the Web', *McKinsey Quarterly*, (2), 74–81.

Gross, A.C., Banting, P.M., Meredith, L.N., and Ford, I.D. (1993), *Business Marketing*, Boston, MA: Houghton Mifflin Co.

Hagel III, J. and Armstrong, A.G. (1997), 'Net Gain: Expanding Markets Through Virtual Communities', *McKinsey Quarterly*, (1), 140–153.

Hagel III, J. and Rayport, J.F. (1997), 'The Coming Battle for Customer Information', *Harvard Business Review*, 75 (1), 53–60.

Håkansson, H. (1980), 'Marketing Strategies in Industrial Markets', *European Journal of Marketing*, 14 (5/6), 365–376.

Håkansson, H. and Snehota, I. (1995), *Developing Relationships in Business Networks*, London, UK: Routledge

Hall, R. (1996), *Organizations – Structures, Processes and Outcomes*, Upper Saddle River, NJ: Prentice Hall.

Helmstetter, G. and Metivier, P. (2000), *Affiliate Selling*, New York, NY: John Wiley & Sons.

IDC (International Data Corporation) (1999), *Affiliate Marketing: The Enablers*, Market Report #19891, Framingham, MA.

Jacobides, M.G. and Croson, D.C. (2001), 'Information Policy: Shaping the Value of Agency Relationships', *Academy of Management Review*, 26 (2), 202–223.

Johnson, G. and Scholes, K. (1998), *Exploring Corporate Strategy*, Hertfordshire, UK: Prentice Hall Europe.

Junghagen, S. (ed.) (1995), *Nyttoskapande med tele- och datakommunikation – en kunskapsöversikt*, Research Report, Umeå, Sweden: Umeå School of Business and Economics.

Junghagen, S. (1998), *Strategiska förhållningssätt till informationsteknik i små företag*, PhD diss, Umeå, Sweden: Umeå University.

Junghagen, S. (1999), *Nyttan av IT – i småföretagarens ögon*, Stockholm, Sweden: NUTEK.

Jupiter Communications (1998), *Pricing Strategies*, Strategic Planning Services Report, July, New York, NY.

Jupiter Communications (1998b), *Affiliate Programmes: Increasing Sales Through Tiered Compensation and Service*, Strategic Planning Services Report, December, New York, NY.

Jupiter Communications (2000), *Online Advertising Through 2005*, Vision Report, August, New York, NY.

Jupiter Communications (2000b), *European Online Advertising*, Jupiter Report, September, New York, NY.

Jupiter Media Metrix (2001), *Rapid Consolidation Dramatically Narrows Number of Companies Controlling Time Controlling Time Spent Online*, www.jmm.com, 4 June.

Kavanagh, M. (1999), 'Amazon Combats Concern over "Feature Placements"', *Marketing Week*, 18 February.

Kelly, K. (1998), *New Rules for the New Economy*, London, UK: Fourth Estate.

Kjærsdam, F. (2000), 'Dot-com i sorte tal på 6 måneder', *Børsen*, 31 October.

Knowledge Foundation (2001), *Mission: Get Ahead*, Stockholm, Sweden: The Knowledge Foundation.

Levine, R., Locke, C., Searls, D., and Weinberger, D. (2000), *The Cluetrain Manifesto*, Cambridge, MA: Perseus Books.

Levinthal, D. (1988), 'A Survey of Agency Models of Organizations', *Journal of Economic Behavior & Organization*, **9** (2), 153–185.

Lindstrom, M. (2001), *Etailhandel: Clicks, Bricks and Brands*, Copenhagen, DK: Børsens Forlag.

Maloney, L. (2001), 'Affiliate Marketing Programmes That Click Can Add Value Without Costs to Websites', *Nation's Restaurant News,* June 4.

McCarthy, J.E. (1960), *Basic Marketing – A Managerial Approach,* Homewood, IL: Richard Irwin.

Mintzberg, H., Ahlstrand, B., and Lampel, J. (1998), *Strategy Safari*, Hemel Hempstead, UK: Prentice Hall.

Nelson, E. and O'Connell, V. (2001), 'P&G-Viacom Deal to Provide Advertising Across Divisions', *Wall Street Journal Europe*, 31 May.

Neubert, O. (2000), 'Resultat-afregning for Internet-markedsføring', *Erhvervsbladet*, 12 October.

Nonaka, I. and Takeuchi, H. (1995), *The Knowledge-Creating Company: How Japanese Companies Create the Dynamics of Innovation,* New York, NY: Oxford University Press.

Ogilvy, J. (1990), 'This Postmodern Business', *Marketing and Research Today*, Feb.

Pascale, R.T., Millemann, M., and Gioja, L. (2000), *Surfing the Edge of Chaos: The Laws of Nature and the New Laws of Business*, London, UK: Texere Publishing.

Peppers, D. and Rogers, M. (1995), 'A New Marketing Paradigm: Share of Customer, Not Market Share', *Planning Review*, **23** (2), 14–18.

Pfeffer, J. and Salancik, G.R. (1978), *The External Control of Organizations: A Resource Dependence Perspective*, London, UK: Harper & Row.

Pine, B.J., Peppers, D., and Rogers, M. (1995), 'Do You Want to Keep Your Customers Forever?' *Harvard Business Review*, **73** (2), 103–113.

Porter, M.E. (1980), *Competitive Strategy: Techniques for Analyzing Industries and Competitors*, New York, NY: The Free Press.

Ray, M.L. (1973), 'Communication and the Hierarchy of Effects', in Clarke, P. (ed.), *New Models for Mass Communication Research*, Beverly Hills, CA: Sage, pp. 147–176.

Schram, W. (1955), *The Process and Effect of Mass Communication*, Champaign, IL: University of Illinois Press.

Shapiro, C. and Varian, H. (1999), *Information Rules – A Strategic Guide to the Network Economy*, Boston, MA: Harvard Business School Press.

Silverstein, B. (2001), 'Developing Internet Partnerships', *Direct Marketing*, **63** (11), 33–43.

Sommer, N. (2001), 'Kan bannerreklamerne slå igen?', *Børsens Nyhedsmagasin*, 2 April.

Spector, R. (2000), *Amazon.com Get Big Fast: Inside the Revolutionary Business Model that Changed The World*, London, UK: Random House.

Stabell, C.B. and Fjeldstad, Ø.D. (1998), 'Configuring Value for Competitive Advantage: On Chains, Shops, and Networks', *Strategic Management Journal*, **19** (5), 413–437.

Strauss, J. and Frost, R. (1999), *Marketing on the Internet: Principles of Online Marketing*, Upper Saddle River, NJ: Prentice Hall.

UCLA (2001) *The UCLA Internet Report 2001: 'Surveying the Digital Future'*, Research Report, Los Angeles, CA: UCLA Center for Communication Policy.

Varian, H.R. (1998), 'Markets for Information Goods', *www.sims.berkely.edu*, Berkely, CA: University of California.

Vaughn, R. (1980), 'How Advertising Works: A Planning Model', *Journal of Advertising Research*, **20** (5), 27–33.

Warner, B. (1999), 'Your Ad Here', *The Standard (www.thestandard.com)*, 17 September.

Webster, F.E. and Wind, Y. (1972), 'A General Model of Organizational Buying Behavior', *Journal of Marketing*, **36** (2), 12–19.

Wernerfelt, B. (1984), 'A Resource Based View of the Firm', *Strategic Management Journal*, **5** (2), 171–180.

Williamson, O.E. (1981), 'Economics of Organization: The Transaction Cost Approach', *American Journal of Sociology*, **87** (3), 548–577.

Zaichkowsky, J.L. (1986), 'Conceptualizing Involvement', *Journal of Advertising*, **15** (2), 4–14.

Zyman, S. (1999), *The End of Marketing as We Know It*, London, UK: HarperCollins.

Index